The Investment Writing Handbook

Founded in 1807, John Wiley & Sons is the oldest independent publishing company in the United States. With offices in North America, Europe, Australia, and Asia, Wiley is globally committed to developing and marketing print and electronic products and services for our customers' professional and personal knowledge and understanding.

The Wiley Finance series contains books written specifically for finance and investment professionals as well as sophisticated individual investors and their financial advisors. Book topics range from portfolio management to e-commerce, risk management, financial engineering, valuation, and financial instrument analysis, as well as much more.

For a list of available titles, visit our Web site at www.WileyFinance.com.

The Investment Writing Handbook

How to Craft Effective Communications to Investors

ASSAF KEDEM

WILEY

Library of Congress Cataloging-in-Publication Data:

Names: Kedem, Assaf, 1973– author.
Title: The investment writing handbook : how to craft effective
   communications to investors / by Assaf Kedem.
Description: Hoboken, New Jersey : John Wiley & Sons, Inc., [2018] | Series:
   Wiley finance series | Includes index. |
Identifiers: LCCN 2017057969 (print) | LCCN 2017059128 (ebook) | ISBN
   9781119356738 (pdf) | ISBN 9781119356745 (epub) | ISBN 9781119356806
   (oBook) | ISBN 9781119356721 (cloth)
Subjects: LCSH: Investment advisors. | Investment advisors—Marketing. |
   Business communication. | Finance—Authorship.
Classification: LCC HG4621 (ebook) | LCC HG4621 .K43 2018 (print) | DDC
   808.06/6332—dc23
LC record available at https://lccn.loc.gov/2017057969

For my parents, Ann and Gideon
my sister, Galit
and my love, Erika

"You must feel not that you want to write but that you have to."
—Christopher Hitchens, *Letters to a Young Contrarian*

Contents

Preface

Investors are dear to my heart: big and small, sophisticated and simple, learned and lay. I write for them daily. They return the favor by mostly reading what I write (or so I hope), keeping me plenty occupied and furnishing my paycheck.

So it's fitting that I should start by begging for investors' forgiveness: This book, alas, is not for them. It's for those who *write* for them. Yes, the writers who develop investment literature and communications on behalf of financial-services firms. You know who you are, dear writers. Know that I toil among you.

You may be a staff writer of an investment firm or a creative-services agency catering to such a firm. You may be a freelancer. Either way, you would typically be writing on behalf of a firm or investment professional—a portfolio manager, chief investment officer, product manager, economist, analyst, advisor, or anyone in a money-management, investor-relations or client-service capacity.

That's not to say investment professionals can't write themselves. There are many who possess financial *and* writing talent—who have the capacity to manage portfolios and products, analyze markets, manage client accounts, or serve in related functions—and write terrific, informative prose for their investors. But since there are also mortals who can't do both at the same time and do them well, there's usually a corporate job out there for the dedicated writer—likely you. Yet if you happen to be an investment professional in need of a handbook to aid in your own writing, then this book is for you, too.

Gore Vidal once said that one should write a book one wishes one read oneself. I certainly wished I had a single comprehensive handbook on how to write for the investor during my many years in the business. Absent such a manual or any formal instruction, I had no choice but to acquire knowledge through trial and error, or what some would proverbially dub the School of Hard Knocks. In the hopes of allowing others to benefit from my experience, I resolved to pen this guide for those in need of structured orientation to this specialized line of work. They include the young and intrepid who venture to join the professional circle of investment writers—and could now learn in just a few hours' worth of reading what took yours truly the better part of 20 years.

My undulating career history has taken me through several major Wall Street firms. This history has been at once a challenge and a blessing. Life isn't all smooth sailing in an industry predisposed to economic gyrations. But it is always riveting—and I have tremendous gratitude for the experience each of my employers has afforded me. Collectively, they have perched me atop a vantage point from which to survey the competitive landscape. The view I've gained is panoramic, the result of diverse exposure to writing and communication practices at an array of marquee institutions with global reach. And I would like to believe that I am now in a position to share with you the best I've encountered.

I could have given up somewhere along the way during the difficult times, but I kept coming back for more. As a writer at the epicenter of periodic, nerve-testing turbulence, I was susceptible to any epiphany that would have led me astray—say, to become a peddler of herbal remedies or the founder of a Neapolitan gelato shop. (Such a career change would have also made for a very different kind of book.) Yet I cannot lay claim to such a revelation. Instead I stayed the course, for I found it intellectually stimulating and professionally rewarding.

It's satisfying to have an investment professional tell me, "You captured exactly what I wanted to say—and said it better than I ever could." Better yet, as a communicator, I find it gratifying to be part of a broader effort that leads to winning a new mandate, to asset inflows into an investment vehicle benefiting clients, or to the provision of useful and timely information to investors in need.

If this book helps bring you closer to even one such moment in your career, then it's been worth it to me.

Introduction: For Whom Is This Handbook, and Why?

In an inconspicuous corner of the investment business, there's a valuable circle of professionals having nothing to do with managing money. Rather than making investments, they make sentences. Armed with a facility for language, they pen literature and communications for the consumption of millions of investors—private and institutional—who entrust portfolio managers, advisors, and consultants with trillions of dollars in assets. Their words can sway investors' opinions, shape their attitudes, affect their decisions, and drive their behavior.

These are the industry's investment writers. This handbook is for them primarily—though not exclusively. It is intended for anyone tasked with the responsibility of writing for the investor. There are many, which is why this book is called *The Investment **Writing** Handbook* rather than *The Investment **Writer's** Handbook*. Still, to understand the context of this craft, it's worth highlighting the dedicated writers for whom this book is chiefly intended.

Investment writers are an ultra-specialized class of communicators in a niche of the third degree. They are writers of financial services. They serve a well-defined segment of that industry dealing exclusively with investments. And, within that segment, they write for what is known as the "buy side," which comprises firms that purchase and sell securities on behalf of investors for money management.

Investment writers have counterparts on the "sell side," which includes brokerage houses and investment banks that underwrite securities, offer public analyst recommendations for them, and publish research. This book is also for them and offers plenty of principles applicable to their business.

Don't take these über-niche writers for a paltry bunch. The investment industry, which plays a major role in the global economy and financial markets, employs bevies of them—staff writers, freelancers, and external agency personnel—who churn out content for a range of communications. At year-end 2016, Cerulli Associates estimated the U.S. investment market alone at nearly $41 trillion in assets[1] that are professionally managed by hundreds of firms on behalf of thousands of institutions and millions of households. These investors include mass-market (retail) investors and wealthy individuals, retirement-plan participants, sponsors of government and corporate retirement plans, endowments, foundations, sovereign wealth funds, insurance companies, and other institutions that invest money.

Since the investment business isn't one of materials but one of ideas, analysis, and consultation, virtually all firms—from hedge funds and family offices to large wealth and asset managers—need to communicate regularly to their clients and place a premium on such communication. So do consultancies and research firms, as well as third-party intermediaries that offer the products of investment firms.

Investment writers are the thought synthesizers and mouthpieces of investment professionals and corporate executives. Often as ghostwriters, and in addition to authoring marketing communications, they help articulate the viewpoints, analyses, and prognostications of chief executive officers, chief investment officers, portfolio managers, product managers, client-account managers, economists, analysts, investment advisors, investor-relations staff, and others. Many investment professionals also carve out precious time between other duties to write themselves—without the help of dedicated writers—and communicate to investors or the general public about investment issues. This handbook is for them, too, for when they don the writer's cap.

All this is to say that investment writing is a vital function in a business whose proposition is intellectual rather than physical. It is performed by seasoned practitioners serving a sizable contingent of firms and their clients, with trillions of dollars in managed assets at stake. Like other disciplines, it has conventions, processes, recommended practices, and complexities. Like other art forms, it involves creativity. And, like other weighty professions, it requires training through experience. That's enough to warrant a handbook, so here you have one. Brace yourself for the journey.

NOTE

1. Cerulli Associates, "The State of U.S. Retail and Institutional Asset Management—2017."

Acknowledgments

This is my opportunity to heap appreciation upon the thanks I already owe the two individuals who brought me into this world. With fierce encouragement, my parents have been pleading with me to write a book—*any* book—for years now.

A novelist I am not. A memoir would have been too presumptuous by fault of my relative youth. But since investment writing is what I do by day (and sometimes night), why not share what I've learned in my professional life to benefit others? I met a receptive listener in John Deremigis, who devoted his generous time to studying my ideas for this book, introduced me to Wiley, and helped usher my career-long wish from the obscurity of a pipe dream to the doorstep of reality.

I'd be remiss to not mention Orily Pratt, who was the first to take a chance on me despite my rudimentary qualifications, furnish me with a launch pad to the world, and demonstrate more than anyone that managers can and should be talent nurturers. Sending me off to my first senior job, she inscribed a copy of *Alice in Wonderland* to me with characteristic flair: "Good luck is wished upon those whose success is unsure," she wrote, "but since that's clearly not the case with you, I trust that *Alice* will help spice up your journey, make it pleasurable, and afford you counsel in times of doubt." I can't think of a better nurturer.

Then there are those who opened their doors, hearts, and checkbooks while excusing my quirks; those who have offered mentorship and friendship; and those to whom I owe my professional experience over the years. I particularly want to acknowledge—in no particular order—Diane Gargiulo and her associates, Robert Bilse, Betsy Perlman, Jeanne Sdroulas, Brian Steel, Chris Poe, Daniel Donnelly, Trudi Baldwin, Chris Thabet, Bernard Del Rey, Jay Rubin, Judith Jones, Robert Noltenmeier, Robert Bosselman, Joe Kolman, Dorothy Nickelson, Matthew Stadtmauer, Jennifer Babsin, Avi Sharon, Pat David, Joe Gavin, Ana Duarte-McCarthy, and Robert Brazier.

Regrettably, I haven't room to list the many more colleagues for whom I had the privilege to write. But I hope they find a token of my gratitude in the words I've left behind.

Notwithstanding the well-worn adage that a book should not be judged by its cover, I credit my friend Tim Cilurso for his visually creative gateway to these words.

Thanks to Evan Gordon, Michelle DeWitt, Wim Vandenhoeck, Vered Zimmerman, and Brian Levitt, who shared their perspectives with me for this project.

Finally, the Bouers, the Rothbaums, and the extended Kedem and Rabbani families have been New York's gift to me since Day One. And it is Erika Woods, my sounding board and veritable rock, whose unfailingly wise counsel I could not do without.

About the Author

Assaf Kedem is an award-winning writer who, over a career spanning two decades, has served in a range of communication roles at global financial firms, including JPMorganChase, Merrill Lynch, BlackRock, Citigroup, Morgan Stanley, AllianceBernstein, Kohlberg Kravis Roberts (KKR), MSCI, and OppenheimerFunds. He is also an adjunct professor of writing and communications at New York University's master's program in public relations and corporate communication, and he lectures periodically at The Summit for Asset Management (TSAM), a global congress and series of events featuring educational discussions about the investment industry. Assaf earned an M.S. in strategic communications from Columbia University and a B.A. in economics and management from the Israel Institute of Technology (Technion).

The Investment Writing Handbook

CHAPTER 1

The Building Blocks of Investment Writing

Having selected this of all handbooks, you likely have a firm grasp—or at least a general idea—of what investment writing is. Still, I'll offer a definition to frame what this book will cover.

WHAT'S INVESTMENT WRITING ALL ABOUT?

In the broadest terms, investment writing is the development of copy that serves one or more of the following aims:

1. To inform or educate current and prospective investors
2. To offer or promote an investment product or service
3. To cultivate relationships with investors and their advisors and consultants, influence their opinions, manage their expectations, and address their concerns

For the first you may write research papers, commentary, periodical reports, and explanatory literature intended to demystify investment concepts, introduce new ideas and perspectives, and keep investors apprised of issues relating to their investments. The second requires writing explicitly to promote a firm's investment capabilities and can take the form of marketing literature (such as brochures), product fact sheets, case studies, pitch books, presentations, and proposals (RFPs). And the third requires ongoing communication, such as in the form of letter correspondences, newsletters, and various forms of commentary. This book will explain how to write for each.

But first, there are general principles that apply to all forms of investment writing across the board, which usually revolve around answering any combination of the following core questions:

1. What is the most pertinent information the investor needs to know?
2. How is the investor affected?
3. What analyses, insights, or strategies can the investment professional offer?
4. What is the problem the investment professional wishes to solve and the solution proposed?
5. How can the investor benefit?

With the answers to those questions in mind, remember that good investment writing isn't just about grammatical and syntactical correctness, clarity, proper spelling and punctuation, and elegant prose. It's about the practical usefulness of your content. To write well for the investor, you need to offer utility. In turn, the investor ought to be able to absorb what you write with ease, efficiency, and persuasion, and use it to make informed and timely decisions.

This may sound obvious and straightforward, but in practice, investment writing requires striking an elusive balance on several fronts. It draws from journalistic principles, yet isn't quite journalism as it involves more than just reporting. It is often deployed in the service of marketing but shouldn't always be written promotionally. It's a form of strategic communication to drive business but should also provide valuable information the investor can use. It entails modulating your style and vocabulary to suit different levels of audience sophistication. And it needs to comply with stringent regulatory requirements that are tricky to fulfill: You can be predictive but not promissory; you need to be specific enough for clarity but general enough to accommodate exceptions; and nuance can spell the difference between legal compliance and legal liability.

What does all this mean in practice? Throughout this book, we'll explore the range of principles embodied in effective investment writing—and how to apply them in practice.

APPLYING JOURNALISTIC PRINCIPLES TO INVESTMENT WRITING

Some of the narrative forms of investment writing—such as market commentary, research papers, news items, and feature stories—resemble journalism and apply three journalistic principles in particular:

1. The Five Ws and the Pyramid Principle
2. Inquisitiveness
3. Proactive idea generation

The Five *Ws* and the Pyramid Principle

Journalism's famous Five Ws (also known as Five Ws and One *H*) cover the essentials of storytelling and can afford you a checklist of what to include in your writing—or at least help you structure an outline for your piece:

1. Who or what is it about?
2. What happened (what's the story)?
3. When did it take place?
4. Where did it take place?
5. Why did it happen?
6. How did it happen?

Another rule is what author Barbara Minto coined the Pyramid Principle:[1] a logical way of sorting out, grouping, and summarizing ideas, and then formulating them cohesively and comprehensibly in writing. The pyramid is a metaphor for a top-down structure: You begin with a broad idea that encapsulates the ideas that follow, which themselves summarize or preface the subsequent ideas on which you intend to elaborate. To put it differently, you begin at the highest level of abstraction and then proceed downward, delving into more detail and thus creating a logical flow that is easy for the reader to follow and grasp.

For an example of the Five Ws, One *H*, and Pyramid Principle in practice, consider InvestorPro, Inc., an imaginary asset-management firm whose mutual funds and annuities received favorable rankings in the surveys of Ratings & Co., a fictitious investment ratings agency. Suppose the firm wishes to announce these rankings to investors in the form of a news feature on its website or a press release. The first paragraph of such an announcement could begin in general terms to introduce the subject and answer questions 1 through 4 of the Five Ws:

InvestorPro's mutual funds and annuities achieved high rankings among competitors based on factors that include investment returns, risk management, and fees, according to a leading independent rating agency.

The second paragraph would proceed with greater specificity and provide context:

> *Our mutual funds ranked among the top 10 in one-year perfor-mance in 2017 among 60 fund families in the latest Ratings & Co. Fund Family survey on the basis of performance data. The top-10 rating continues a positive trend moving the funds from 30th place in 2015 to 11th in 2016 and now to 10th in 2017. InvestorPro also ranked fourth in the individual one-year Alternative Asset category, which includes our multi-asset fund series, the Alpha Plus funds.*

The third paragraph could add further detail on the reasons for the strong performance, answer questions 5 and 6 of the Five Ws, and take the opportunity to shed some light on the firm's capabilities without sounding too self-congratulatory:

> *The Ratings & Co. survey reflects strong performance across InvestorPro's mutual fund family. We attribute our steady advance in the rankings largely to proprietary investment research con-ducted by more than 150 portfolio managers, research analysts, and traders in our asset-management business.*

Inquisitiveness

Quality investment writing isn't only the product of one's facility with lan-guage. Like journalism, it also demands a reporter's mentality: the instinct to seek out a story, identify and pursue experts from whom to obtain infor-mation, conduct an effective interview—sometimes with little context or background—and dig for what's interesting and new.

There is no shortage of stories to be found in the world of financial mar-kets and metrics, which investment professionals analyze to make decisions on behalf of their clients. For example, numerical information—whether in economic data, corporate balance sheets, security prices and valuation models, market behavior, or investment performance—can be verbalized in relatable narratives.

What's investment writing if not the story behind the numbers? The writer should be eager to canvass those numbers for a good scoop—perhaps with the help of an analyst—and make a compelling observation that would engage the investor. Is there newfound correlation between two datasets that could point to a relationship between them? Are historical figures available to provide a clearer frame of reference or support a thesis?

Figure 1.1, which packs a punch of dense quantitative information, is a case in point. It shows how valuations of two imaginary groups of

FIGURE 1.1   Investment writers are often faced with dense information...

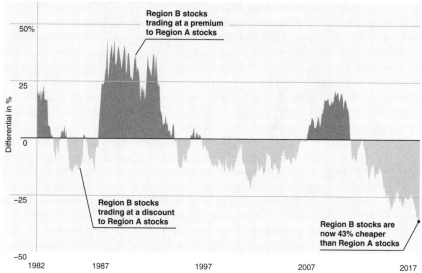

Region B stocks Appear Attractively Valued Relative to Their Region A Counterparts
Cyclically Adjusted Price/Earnings (CAPE) vs. Region A (1982–2017)

stocks—one from "Region A," and the other from "Region B"—have historically fared in comparison with one another.

To illustrate their relative performance, Figure 1.1 depicts the differentials between the stock market indexes representing two of these respective regions—we'll call them the Region A Index and the Region B Index—over a period of 35 years, from 1982 to 2017. (The valuations are represented as the cyclically adjusted price/earnings ratio of each index.) The dark-shaded areas indicate when Region B's stocks were trading at a premium to Region A's stocks, whereas the light-shaded areas point to when they were trading at a discount.

Figure 1.1 shows that in 2017, Region B's stocks, as a group, were 43 percent cheaper than their Region A counterparts, with the implication that they were attractively priced relative to Region A's stocks that year. A writer could look at this figure and ask: Is there another data point that could further bolster the case for why Region B stocks may look comparatively cheap?

The answer is yes: One could also examine the average differential over the entire period to get a better sense of proportion. As it turns out, Region B's stocks had been trading at an average discount of 10 percent to Region A's stocks all along, over the same period. This figure adds a

FIGURE 1.2 . . . and they can make a big difference in pursuing more detail about a story to add richer perspective.

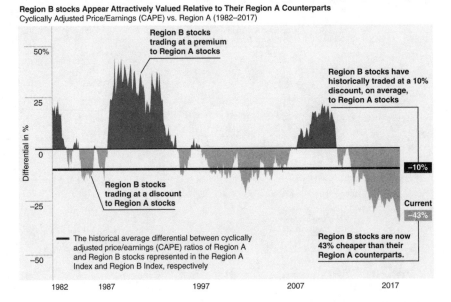

Region B stocks Appear Attractively Valued Relative to Their Region A Counterparts
Cyclically Adjusted Price/Earnings (CAPE) vs. Region A (1982–2017)

historic dimension to the argument. As shown in Figure 1.2, it highlights the 43 percent discount in 2017 as a genuine aberration over such a long time frame—one that could have made an even stronger case at the time for pivoting portfolios toward Region B stocks.

In instances like this, investment writers can make a big difference by pursuing more detail about a story—even if it's a single data point—through further inquiry and investigation.

Proactive Idea Generation

Another journalistic aspect of investment writing is the need for proactive idea generation. Investment professionals embody treasure troves of intellectual capital waiting to be unlocked and shared with the investors they serve. Busy as they are managing money, they may not think to volunteer their knowledge and opinions unless someone solicits them.

It is often the writer's duty to come up with ideas for topics to write about, find appropriate occasions on which to approach and interview the investment professionals, and verbalize their perspectives for the broader public, just like an investigative reporter following exciting leads and examining story angles. Here are some general questions you may ask the investment professionals in your interview:

- How do you view the state of the financial markets?
- What opportunities do you see—and what strategies do you propose to capture them?
- What is your outlook for the period that lies ahead?

Turbulent periods in the financial markets are the classic example of when writers need to take initiative. In such times, portfolio managers become preoccupied with market volatility, yet investors grow concerned amid uncertainty and they thirst for information and points of view. They wish to understand what's causing the tumult and how it might affect their portfolios. They want to know what the portfolio managers think of market developments and how they assess near- and long-term implications and prospects. And they would like the managers to explain what investment strategies they have in place to address the situation. The writer should anticipate these and other questions investors might ask, tap the managers for answers, and craft informative communications on their behalf. I'll address this process in detail in Chapter 5 on developing an architecture of investment content.

THE STRATEGIC PURPOSES OF INVESTMENT WRITING

Journalistic principles are cornerstones of investment writing when it comes to story seeking and storytelling. But investment writing goes beyond journalism in its ultimate goal. Whereas journalism serves to chronicle, expose, and inform—a worthy mission by itself—investment writing is done in the service of an investment management business and its clients and therefore must be strategic. "Strategic" means objective-driven writing, namely: writing with a purpose. And just what might that purpose be? That depends on where the firm's objectives intersect with the investor's need in the context of a specific communication.

Here are some of the most common strategic communication objectives of investment firms:

1. **Acquiring new investors and retaining existing ones**

    Investment firms rely on the written word to win new business (i.e., raise capital or gather assets to be managed) and retain it. That's because their products and services are intellectual rather than physical, and they are based on ideas, strategies, consultation, research, and analysis.

    Additionally, investment management is an event-driven business, as capital markets are dynamic and continually affected by current affairs. This means that communication does not end once an investor signs on; it is required practice throughout the client relationship—one that demands continuing effort—as investors need to be educated and apprised on a regular basis and their concerns addressed.

2. **Cultivating relations with intermediaries**

Investment products and services are often distributed through interlocutors: the advisors and consultants who work with private and institutional investors, provide them with counsel and guidance, help them select investment managers, and recommend specific products.

As a writer on behalf of an investment firm, your job is to communicate not only to investors—but also to the intermediary community that serves them and is an important channel through which to deliver your firm's products and services.

3. **Fulfilling regulatory requirements**

Some investor communications are compulsory by regulatory requirements. Countries differ in their regulatory regimes, but in the United States, for example, registered investment companies must produce periodical communications to shareholders of mutual funds detailing performance information. They typically pair their performance reports with descriptive commentary containing qualitative and numerical explanations, analyses, and perspectives (see Chapter 5, Part 5).

Investment firms must also inform shareholders of certain changes to their fund, or ask them to consider—and vote on—proposals relating to their fund, such as mergers, acquisitions, or changes to a fund's structure. (Vote solicitations are communicated in the form of written proxies, which provide information that is necessary for shareholders to make an informed decision and cast their ballot.)

When communicating to fulfill a regulatory requirement, avoid the mentality of "going through the motions" just to check a box, and try not to write in a manner that is merely perfunctory as a legal disclaimer would sound (see section titled "On Using Jargon" in Chapter 4). Approach the task not with the sense that it is a regulatory burden, but rather with the realization that every communication is a touchpoint with your client and an opportunity to illuminate, educate, and engage.

Over the next chapters, we'll take a closer look at writing to achieve these strategic objectives.

NOTE

1. Barbara Minto, *The Pyramid Principle: Logic in Writing and Thinking* (London, England: Minto International, Inc., 1987).

CHAPTER 2

Writing for Investor Acquisition and Retention

L et's face it: Sales are the lifeblood of any business, and investment writing is one of the communication tools at a financial firm's disposal for winning new investors and keeping existing ones. But the sales proposition isn't always as straightforward as an advertisement.

Why? Partially because many investment offerings are too complex to be reduced or stripped down to the sound bite of an ad, but mainly because investors entrust very large sums of money with those who manage it—and their goals vary. It's not enough to pitch a litany of product specifications, however competitive, and expect the investor's needs to fall in line. Often, you will need to frame your proposition as a solution to a common problem, or as a component of a broader strategy to help investors meet their objectives. Forget about approaching them with *your* agenda; it is *theirs* that should—and will—take center stage.

To do so, remind yourself of the three general types of investors you might be addressing and their common characteristics and potential goals.

1. *Individual investors of ordinary income* make up the largest audience and number in the millions. Known as retail or mass-market investors, they range from retirement-plan participants to those who invest independently. Many possess only rudimentary investment literacy and require fundamental education about investment concepts. Their objectives may be short-term and more tactical (e.g., an opportunistic foray into the market to "make a hit"); medium-term (like growing capital to finance education or a major purchase); or long-term (such as building a nest egg for retirement).

    Some retail investors are more aggressive and tolerant of risks; others are more conservative. They may invest with a firm on their own accord or through an advisor. Consider those advisors when you write: As the ones who have direct, face-to-face relationships with their clients—and who often make investment decisions on their behalf—advisors are gatekeepers in positions of critical influence. If they believe your literature is valuable for their clients, they'll share it with them. The same applies to advisors of high-net-worth investors as well as to institutional investor consultants.

2. *High-net-worth investors* are affluent individuals and families who possess a higher amount of investable assets. They, too, have short-, medium-, and long-term investment goals. Some seek to grow their wealth, whereas others are more financially conservative and merely wish to preserve it by keeping pace with inflation. Some have philanthropic causes they would like to fund. Many seek counsel to help navigate the complexities of managing their trusts, their estates, the wealth they amass through business ventures, and the transfer of wealth within their families across generations. There are investment firms that take a holistic approach to these issues by serving as convenient one-stop shops for all wealth-related affairs—and providing a variety of services to tackle each of them.

   High-net-worth investors who enlist the services of an investment firm may expect those services to be delivered on their personal terms and adapted to suit granular needs. For instance, they could require an investment strategy to be tailored to certain tax-management or accounting parameters. They may even want the managers they hire to work in coordination and consultation with their personal tax attorneys and accountants.

3. *Institutional investors* include corporate and government sponsors of employee retirement plans, as well as endowments, foundations, sovereign wealth funds, financial institutions (such as insurance companies), government agencies, and other organizations.

   Institutions are typically the largest and most sophisticated investors. They employ seasoned professionals whose responsibility is to make investment decisions, often with the external help of investment-management firms. As a writer in the service of such firms, you'd be addressing those professionals (say, the chief investment officer of a university endowment), who are steeped in highly technical knowledge of the financial markets and the mechanics of investing. Weigh this factor in your vocabulary, style, and content when addressing them. (In Chapter 4, I'll elaborate on ways to modulate your writing style for different audiences.)

   Institutions have wide-ranging goals. For example, sponsors of defined-benefit retirement plans (in which the employer promises a specified pension payment to employees) need to fund payouts to current and future retirees. They do so by making monetary contributions to their plans and investing those contributions for returns. Their investment objectives may include capital appreciation, income generation, and managing the volatility of their portfolios' values.

Endowments and foundations need to continue funding their missions in a sustainable way—whether by growing the capital they receive from donations while maintaining a certain amount of liquidity (i.e., cash or cash-equivalent assets); by securing a steady stream of income; or by managing portfolio volatility.

Sovereign wealth funds, which are state-owned, may wish to grow their asset base in order to protect and stabilize national budgets, or to help finance social programs and economic development in their home countries. Some may elect to invest domestically rather than overseas; others may be high risk-takers and wish to sacrifice liquidity for higher investment returns.

Insurance companies accumulate significant amounts of cash from the money they collect in premiums. They may use this cash to invest in assets that support their policy reserves, which are used to pay obligations to policyholders as they become due.[1]

And the list goes on.

These broad descriptions of investor audiences are, of course, generalizations. You may encounter exceptions to them or additional specifics they do not include. Regardless, the point is evident: Investors vary—and their goals are all over the map.

Therefore, to write strategically for the purpose of acquiring new investors or retaining existing ones, it's clear why you would want to express your proposition as a solution that would speak to the respective goals and challenges of each audience.

FRAMING YOUR INVESTMENT PROPOSITION AS THE SOLUTION TO A PROBLEM

Here's a hypothetical example that's typical enough to serve as an archetype of situation you might encounter. Suppose you're developing marketing literature to promote a strategy for investing in stocks of companies located in economically developing regions throughout the world. (For argument's sake, it doesn't matter whether the strategy is delivered through a mutual fund, separately managed account, or other vehicle.) The strategy's objective is to gain attractive returns by investing in companies that have the potential to capitalize on the maturation of their home regions and eventually hit a growth spurt.

There are four steps you could follow to articulate your proposition to the prospective investor:

1. Define your offering.
2. Identify your client's problem.
3. Acknowledge the problem.
4. Frame your offering to address the investor's concerns.

Step 1: Define Your Offering

Once investors take interest in your proposed strategy, they will ask basic questions about the investment philosophy behind it, as well as its process and objectives. For example, they'll want to know how your firm identifies outfits with growth potential. Are you looking to invest in pioneering companies that are introducing new categories of products and creating a market for them that had not existed before? Or companies looking to gain market share within an existing market through some competitive advantage? Or perhaps both? What evaluation metrics do you use in your analytical arsenal to determine which companies are qualified for investment? What annual returns do you seek? (For more on how to best answer these types of questions, refer to Part 1 of Chapter 5 on foundational literature.)

This information is crucial for your investors to know—at least as soon as they begin to inquire further about your investment strategy. Yet the specifics of your offering may not interest them initially, especially if they aren't deliberately pursuing a stock-investing strategy to begin with. What might spark their interest in the first place?

Step 2: Identify Your Client's Problem

To answer this question, imagine your prospective client—a huge government retirement fund. This multibillion-dollar fund was established to pay out pensions to thousands of teachers employed by the public education system of a large U.S. state. The fund's executives, who are the decision-makers, are your audience. They're the ones responsible for running the fund, maintaining its solvency, and determining how to invest its money. They will vet every word you write and run a fine-tooth comb through your proposition.

And they are facing a nightmare. Arithmetic shows that their fund is unable to meet its future obligations. In other words, the fund's current assets, accumulated through contributions made by the state over the years, aren't sufficient to keep pace with what it will need to disburse in future retirement benefits. At stake is the livelihood of thousands of retirees. It's the pension money of all state teachers—those who have already retired and those who are working but will come to depend on it in their twilight years. (Incidentally, many retirement funds throughout the United States have faced this real-life problem since the financial crisis of 2008–2009. And though this particular problem may no longer be prevalent by the time you read these words, it's an instructive example of the kind of challenges facing institutional investors that you'll invariably find yourself having to address in the literature you write.)

Staring down the barrel of a gaping shortfall, the retirement fund's executives scramble for solutions. They look to hire an investment management firm that will successfully grow the fund's assets through investing, bring its asset/liability mismatch into balance, and attain a surplus of assets as a cushion against future uncertainty. But they also have a checklist of technical requirements for how the fund's investment portfolio should be managed. It needs to achieve potential annual returns within a desired range; it cannot exceed a certain level of risk (expressed in statistical terms as the expected standard deviation of a portfolio's performance); there has to be enough cash on the side as a residual safeguard in case things go wrong; and there are other technical requirements, too.

Now, imagine these executives, preoccupied as they are with their problems, sitting in a boardroom and holding your literature in their hands. They've just read your description of a strategy to invest money in promising companies throughout the developing world. They have reviewed your forceful case for considering this strategy as an opportunity to reap the rewards of businesses that are poised for growth. What now?

They may take immediate interest in your proposition, inquire further, and eventually entrust your firm with the sacred duty of investing the retirement money of their state's teachers. Then again, there's also an understandable chance they'll not be prepared to make the intellectual leap—or take a leap of faith—from the problem they face to the strategy you're proposing. That is, unless you address their problem *first*, show them you fully comprehend the nature of that problem, and couch your investment strategy as a solution.

This is your opportunity to add breadth and depth to your offering by taking a few steps back, sizing it up from afar, and imagining its broader purpose in tackling your client's problem. It's an opportunity to show you genuinely understand the needs of your client and can cater to those needs. If you seize it, you'll distinguish your proposition as coming from a consultative partner—rather than from just another garden-variety vendor of investment products with a sales pitch. In so doing, you'll stand a greater chance of procuring your client's interest.

Step 3: Acknowledge the Problem

Consider prefacing your proposition with a written acknowledgment of the problem and—with the aid of some research—the extent of it across your target market. Such a preface would demonstrate an appreciation of your client and the challenges it faces. In this example, consider the following theoretical opener that acknowledges the problem of funding gaps among public and private retirement funds in the United States:

> *Many defined-benefit retirement funds—public, private single-employer, and private multi-employer—continue to face significant funding shortfalls, even X years after the financial crisis of 2008. For example, state funds still had an aggregate funding gap of more than $X billion at the dawn of [YEAR], according to [YOUR SOURCE OF RESEARCH].*

An opener like this one has the powerful capacity to draw in your prospect, because it immediately couches your offering in relatable context.

Step 4: Frame Your Offering to Address the Investor's Concerns

Next, frame your proposed investment strategy as a solution to your client's problem—or link it directly to your client's goals. You can go about this approach any number of ways. One is to explain how your strategy could fit as a piece in a larger puzzle toward helping your client tackle the challenge at hand. For example, if your client has a diverse portfolio—as many institutional investors do to achieve their objectives—then consider presenting your strategy as complementary to a broader allocation of investments across asset classes and geographic regions, provided that you are able to illustrate the advantages it would bring to your client's portfolio.

In this instance, you may want to show how an investment allocation to companies in developing markets can fortify a portfolio toward reducing the gap between the assets and liabilities of your client's retirement fund. Is there a numerical proxy, such as a regional or industry index of developing-market stocks, that you could use to demonstrate how the companies in which you propose to invest have performed over a certain period? What behavioral characteristics does this index exhibit when compared with indexes of other markets in which your client invests—say, U.S. stocks or bonds?

If you find that the indexes are uncorrelated, then you could make a case for enhancing your client's diversification: By nature, owning a variety of securities that move independently from one another can help offset the inherent volatility of individual holdings. Why would the chief investment officer of a retirement fund care? Perhaps because investing in your strategy would help reduce fluctuations in the value of the fund's portfolio and minimize the risk of widening its asset/liability gap in any given period.

However you choose to articulate your proposition depends on the investment strategy you are attempting to market—and on your client's particular situation and needs. But in any case, before putting pen to paper, ask yourself the very questions your client might ask you and try to answer them as you go along. Put yourself in the shoes of a retirement fund's executive in this example, who might be wondering: "We need a blend of capital appreciation and income that would help us sustain a growing stream of pension payments to our teachers, given longer life expectancies and a larger projected pool of retirees in the years to come. How can you, the investment manager, help us?"

The approach of linking your proposition to the client's objectives applies to any audience—be it retail, high-net-worth, or institutional investors. For example, you can demonstrate how your proposed strategy of investing in companies of developing markets can help build a nest egg for an individual's retirement, or grow capital to fund a charitable cause dear to a philanthropist's heart.

The bottom line? To win over new investors, tie your offering to their objectives and express it in terms of their needs.

INVESTOR RETENTION: IT'S ALL IN THE COMMUNICATION

The sheer act of communicating is essential to retaining investors. Do it regularly—whether the news is positive or negative. The investors who entrusted you with their money may expect to hear from you every so often. If you fail to reach out to them for an extended period, there's a good chance they'll fill the void with their own conjecture. And the last thing you would want is for them to make decisions based on uninformed conclusions.

Also, when it comes to investor retention, remember the renowned Leon Levy, who said that investing is as much a psychological act as an economic one. And why wouldn't it be? With their personal fortunes and financial security on the line, investors are driven not only by financial goals—but also, understandably, by emotions. These emotions can vacillate between fear (whether justified or not) and greed (occasionally at their peril) and could result in impulsive investment decisions, to which human behavior is ever prone.

Case in point: It's not uncommon to witness investors flock in droves to popular investment destinations in heady times, only to panic during a subsequent drawdown, pull back from the market at an inopportune moment, and find in retrospect that they had bought high and sold low. And, as one CEO put it, investors feel the pain of loss more than they do the joy of gain.

Be prepared to address the pitfalls of making rash decisions driven by feelings—especially during turbulent periods. Psychoanalysis and psychotherapy aren't your job. But as an investment writer, you may need to make a strong, rational case—backed by historical data—for the cyclical nature of markets; for the patience that is often required for investments to bear fruit; for the perils in trying to time the market and chase highly performing assets when it's already too late; and for diversification and prudent risk management. Investors will take note.

Take an example in the following hypothetical letter by a firm alerting investors to the possibility of turbulence in the wake of rising interest rates:

> *Subject: How we believe investors should respond to an interest rate hike*
>
> *Dear [NAME]:*
>
> *At its recent meeting, the U.S. Federal Reserve raised the federal funds rate by 0.25%. This increase reflects the Fed's confidence in the U.S. economy, yet it could also trigger some turbulence in the short run as the financial markets digest the news.*
>
> *We encourage you to take market volatility in stride and maintain a long-term perspective on the effect of rate hikes on bonds. Consider that short-term pain could also give way to later gains. Higher interest rates can cause existing bonds that pay lower coupon rates to decrease in market value—but they may also introduce new opportunities for higher income from newly issued bonds.*
>
> *Finally, remember that the primary role of bonds in your portfolio is to serve as a diversifier against sharp swings in the stock market. For more information, read our attached article on market cycles and what higher interest rates mean for your portfolio.*

Indeed, the long view—a common theme of emphasis for investor retention—isn't merely self-serving for investment managers. In plenty of cases, it actually makes a great deal of sense from the investor's perspective on the basis of market history. So here's a suggested philosophy: Don't shy away from pressing investors to do the right thing, even if it also happens to be in your firm's own best interest!

Opportunities for Retentive Communications

Retentive communications can take a number of forms—from periodic commentary or a special research note, to a personal letter to investors authored by a portfolio manager, chief investment officer, or CEO. Market events or changes involving an investment fund, strategy, or portfolio management staff are good opportunities to communicate. So are calendric milestones (such as the middle, end, or beginning of a year) or the major anniversary of a firm's founding, a fund's inception, or a portfolio manager's service.

These occasions provide you with opportunities to engage investors in support of your business through a number of ways:

- Remind investors you're there to continue serving them. (Yes, those who don't give frequent thought to the money they tuck away for long-term financial goals could use an occasional *aide-mémoire* from the professionals who work all year round to manage it.)
- Express your thanks and appreciation for their continued business, trust, and confidence in you.
- Update them regularly on market developments—especially if they are dramatic—and the performance of their portfolios while providing historical context for the numbers.
- Recap your firm's periodic activity and achievements, highlight your performance track record if it's worth pointing out, and take a retrospective opportunity to justify investment decisions, made by the firm on investors' behalf, that paid off.
- Provide your current perspective on, or interpretation of, where things stand with regard to the portfolios you manage or the markets at large.
- Address investors' concerns and offer them reassurances, assuming you feel they are warranted (more on that shortly).
- Articulate your prognostications for what lies ahead.
- Emphasize the teamwork behind the management of your investors' money. Collaboration is an advantage to tout in an intellectually based business and, many would argue, conducive to rigorous research and to making well-rounded investment decisions. Some investors also want to know that they're not just putting their money with a single manager who may not be there in the future, but rather with a team of experienced professionals.
- Take an opportunity to introduce key talent your firm has recently hired toward augmenting its organization.

As an example of many of these retention principles in practice, take Terry Tenure, a lead portfolio manager of the fictitious Small Cap Technology Fund. True to her name, Ms. Tenure has served as head of the fund for

25 years and wishes to acknowledge her quarter-century anniversary with a personal letter to her shareholders.

Here's how such a letter might look:

Dear Shareholder:

Today marks my 25th anniversary as the lead portfolio manager of the Small Cap Technology Fund. It has been a privilege serving you alongside my management team since I took the helm of the fund on [DATE].

At this milestone, here's the most important thing I would like you to know: The approach my team and I take to managing your investment will not change under my supervision. I emphasize this precisely because there are very few things that haven't changed over the past quarter century. Turn back the calendar to 1996, and you'll recall that the Internet was in its infancy. The idea of riding in a self-driving car while dictating instructions to a smartphone was the stuff of science fiction. Fitting a library's worth of books on a chip the size of your fingernail was a pipe dream. Today, both are reality—the products of long-term, game-changing trends in which we have been investing for your benefit all along.

Of course, the past 25 years have been about much more than technological innovation. We've also had to navigate your fund through market turmoil, including the Asian and Russian financial crises of 1997–1998; the collapse of the dot-com bubble in 2000; the Great Recession of 2008–2009; a series of debt crises that shook the European Union from 2011 to 2015; and major geopolitical events, from the September 11 terrorist attacks to the Arab Spring, which has redrawn the Middle East.

All throughout, we've adhered to a single, consistent philosophy in pursuit of opportunity: to discern transformative themes in technology and identify small companies with sustainable business models that are poised to capitalize on these themes and grow. So far we've managed to produce annualized returns of X% since the fund's launch. If you've been invested with the fund since its inception, you have made Y dollars on every dollar you put in.

Over these 25 years, I've personally seen bull and bear markets come and go, and that view has only deepened my appreciation for longevity. Time is what it takes to pinpoint the limited number of exceptional companies that execute their strategies well and deploy capital wisely. Once identified, such companies can help investors fully capitalize on the wealth they create over an extended period. Time is also what allows a portfolio manager to explore and learn, to hone the craft, and to ultimately improve outcomes for shareholders.

Finally, I am just one member of an experienced, thoroughly dedicated group of co-managers and analysts without whom your fund could not have been successful. Aware that you invest to pursue important goals, we do not take the trust you've placed in us for granted. And we will continue working hard to retain that trust by serving as faithful stewards of your capital for as long as we have the honor to invest on your behalf.

With sincere gratitude,

Terry Tenure

Facts Are Key for Reassuring Your Investors

Sometimes, retaining investors will require reassuring them in moments of change or unfavorable circumstances, such as poor market or investment performance, personnel changes, or changes in investment products or strategies. With help from the *Merriam-Webster Dictionary*, the emphasis is on *reassuring*, which is to make someone less afraid, upset, or doubtful—as opposed to *assuring*, which is to tell someone in a very strong and definite way that something will happen or is true. Assurances, to state the obvious, are prohibited for anything the investment manager cannot absolutely guarantee.

One need not expound on the ethical and legal implications of false or misleading reassurances just to retain business. The premise is that writers would practice nothing short of integrity and make every effort to conform to ethical standards and regulatory requirements in their communications (more on the legal aspects of investment writing in Chapter 7).

Yet the topic of how to reassure investors is an important one to address—even more so in the aftermath of the financial crisis of 2008–2009, which left firms and their investors with sharp losses and put a dent in the industry's credibility. Few organizations phrased it better than the CFA Institute in its open letter to the investment management profession, dated May 2016:

[M]uch of the economic damage due to the global financial crisis has been repaired. Yet the reputation of the financial services sector remains at a critical low, leaving our stakeholders—especially the workers, retirees and taxpayers we serve—understandably ambivalent about their futures.

The question before the house is this: What would pass for a credible way to assuage investors' concerns, allay their doubts, or overcome their objections?

If it is to be effective, your reassuring message should ideally have two characteristics:

1. *It should be anchored in at least one fact.* It's usually not enough to proffer some general wisdom, personal belief, or a clever variation of "everything is going to be okay" for just any investor to accept uncritically, take on faith, or embrace as a form of consolation. When investors ask, "Why should we keep our money with you?" they expect an incisive, defensible appeal—preferably one that could marshal incontrovertible evidence as its basis. And since facts are verifiable, they can bolster your credibility.

   The fact you choose to cite in your reassurance doesn't need to guarantee a positive future outcome for the investor. All it needs to do is support your reassuring claim. It could be a historical account, a bellwether, a telltale sign, a small proof point in the service of a broader argument, a tangible and perhaps quantifiable measure of your capabilities as an investment manager, or your firm's demonstrated successes.

2. *It should make a sensible interpretation or value judgment of that fact.* When presenting facts to support your reassurance, make certain that your view as to why the investor should be reassured is backed by sound reasoning and introduces a valid takeaway for the investor to consider.

The moral barometer for reassuring investors is your conviction: The stronger you feel they would benefit if they stayed with you, the more it would behoove you to reassure them—and not just because of the potential loss of a client. Consider that you would actually be doing your investors a disservice by denying them a reasonable argument for why it might not be beneficial for them to pare their investment, or simply leave you.

   Here are some examples.

Example #1: A Floundering Investment   Suppose that a fund invested a significant share of its assets in the stock of a company that has fallen out of favor because of a spate of depressed earnings over a number of quarters due to declining product sales. The company's stock took a dive and is now off its peak value by roughly 20 percent. If the portfolio managers perceive this decline to be a temporary setback and feel that holding onto the stock could bring rewards in the longer run, it would be justifiable—even warranted—to offer investors a reassuring point of view.

   Such perspective could take the following form:

■ *Contextual introduction:* It can lead with information about the stock's performance history, about when it began to suffer and to what extent, and about the company's declining sales figures.

- *Interpretation:* It could offer a theory, grounded in facts, to explain the cause for the lower product demand the company is experiencing. For example, are there numerical indicators suggesting a sluggish economic climate that might have contributed to the decline in sales? Are the company's peers undergoing similar struggles, suggesting a broader slowdown across the board having nothing to do with the quality of the particular company in question?
- *Reassurance:* It can then state the portfolio managers' upbeat projection about the company's future based on promising facts, such as its historical trajectory, track record of earnings, or market penetration; the quality of its management team; or the vital role its products serve. It could conclude by citing these facts as promising underpinnings that may not be reflected in the share price, that would potentially outlive a slow economic cycle, and that could ultimately produce attractive returns for investors over the long haul.

In general, when delivering bad investment news—whether it's the poor performance of an individual holding in a fund's portfolio, or a negative development for the market at large—the most important thing to remember is this: Don't just report on the news as a journalist would and leave the investor "hanging" in anticipation of future developments. Add to your reporting a value-added explanation of what you believe is the path forward—whether it's a solution to a problem, a longer-term perspective, or any special insight you can provide (more on why in Chapter 5, Part 2).

Example #2: Changes in Personnel Employees come and go, but investment firms are distinct in the way they must handle staff departures vis-à-vis their clients. How so?

Take the packaged-food industry, which operates heavy industrial machinery for mass production, or the petroleum industry, which uses massive rigs for drilling and oil extraction, or chipmakers, which employ high-precision devices for assembling microcircuits and sandwiching them between paper-thin wafers of silicon. What these and other capital-intensive businesses share in common is their utter reliance on equipment, facilities, and infrastructure, which involve major expenditures on procurement and maintenance.

Not so in the investment business. Strip away the basic facilities it *does* use—the office space, furniture, and computers—and you're left with the only true thing running the show, the *raison d'être* of this knowledge-intensive enterprise and the source of its essential value: the money managers. And though computer algorithms play a greater role today in investment management and analytics, money managers remain the indispensable driving force behind key decisions and actions daily. They are the ones bringing to bear individual skills and experience when keeping tabs on market developments, monitoring portfolios, fine-tuning their strategies and developing new ones, devising solutions to investors' problems, communicating to clients, and cultivating relationships with them.

Staff departures are therefore a sensitive matter—especially in the case of a key figure, such as the head of an investment practice, fund, or strategy—that investors and their advisors and consultants would expect you to address with them. And it's not a matter of *if* but *when:* Personnel changes are inevitable, the product of people getting poached by rival firms, wanting to follow a different career path, or simply retiring.

Granted, everyone understands that individuals are at liberty to leave or change jobs. But it's still necessary to reassure them that a staff change would not disrupt the continual management of investors' money or affect it adversely in any way, assuming the firm is in a valid position to do so.

Here's a checklist of seven questions that can help you establish a solid set of facts in support of your reassurance:

1. Is there an established succession plan in case of a professional's departure?
2. Are there immediate replacements of equivalent knowledge and/or experience lined up for a smooth and seamless transition?
3. What are the circumstances of the professional's departure? If you'd prefer not to reveal them, you may simply say that person X is leaving— or has decided to leave—the firm. Yet oftentimes it helps to mention one's intent to simply retire, having reached the natural end of a career. You may also mention one's wish to pursue other endeavors—an understandable reason and perfectly fine justification.
4. What are the successor's professional qualifications and career history, and how many years of experience does that person have? Has the successor already been with the firm and/or team for a while, and if so, how long? Is the successor shifting roles to assume the new position or ascending to it from within a current team?
5. If the professional leaving the firm is part of a team, are there any other remaining team members who are worth highlighting—whether in career history, qualifications, number of years of total experience, or tenure with the firm?
6. If there is no immediate successor, who will assume full and immediate responsibility until a replacement is found? Will that responsibility be shared among a group of individuals or assumed by just one? What are their current functions, career histories, and qualifications, and how many years of experience do they have?

7. Finally, are there any achievements accomplished by the successor or the remaining team members that merit attention and could give investors a sense that their money is in the hands of a competent organization?

For a demonstration, consider this hypothetical message to clients by an imaginary firm following the departure of one if its senior analysts. The circumstances are less than ideal: The analyst suddenly quit and jumped to a competing firm and there is no immediate successor lined up to replace him. Yet fortunately, there are reassuring facts worth citing and positive value judgments to make based on the firm's history, as well as the tenure and experience of its team:

Subject: Commodity Investment Team Announces Management Update

Dear [CLIENT, ADVISOR, or CONSULTANT]:

We are writing to inform you of a personnel change within InvestorPro's commodities investment team.

David Depart, a senior analyst, has left the firm to pursue other opportunities. Mr. Depart covered the agriculture, soft metals, and energy sectors for our global commodity investment strategy.

To ensure the smooth continuity of this strategy and the team's operations, Barbara Boss, who serves as head of the team, has immediately reassigned Mr. Depart's coverage to two other senior analysts on the team until we complete our active search for his replacement. Those analysts are Latoya Loyal and Sam Steadfast, who have 12 and 10 years of experience covering commodities, respectively. Ms. Loyal and Mr. Steadfast have served with the team for the past seven years.

Ms. Boss, a tenured professional with 20 years of investment experienced, joined the team in [YEAR] and continues to assume responsibility for portfolio management. Under her leadership, the team's assets under management have more than doubled, from US$1 billion as of [DATE] to roughly US$2.5 billion today. Previously announced plans to further expand the team remain intact.

Our collaborative approach to investing, which draws on the collective experience and skills of all our team members, has been—and continues to be—the hallmark of InvestorPro since our founding X years ago. It's an approach we've established not only to make better investment decisions, but also to effectively undertake personnel changes like this one. We are confident this approach will continue to benefit our strategies and, in turn, investors like you in the years to come.

Please do not hesitate to contact me should you have any questions.

Sincerely,

[NAME AND TITLE]

What about references in your investment literature to individuals who are no longer with the firm? Do you promptly begin purging your websites, brochures, research papers, and all manner of content? That depends.

To the extent such references are no longer relevant, then yes: In current descriptions of acting personnel, there's no reason to mention anyone whose presence and contributions can only be couched in the past tense. But it's a different matter if the person who left played a major role in the annals of your firm (e.g., as a founder or partner) and you're writing a chronology—say, for the "about us" section of a website, the "company history" section of an RFP response, the "timeline" segment of a brochure, or a video about the firm's history. In that case, it's okay to include a brief mention of a former colleague for integrity's sake, even in just a few words, assuming that person is an essential part of the historical description. Whatever you do, avoid any attempt at rewriting history, which would not go over well with your constituencies.

Example #3: Changes to an Investment Product Investors aren't the only ones susceptible to market whims. So are their gateways to the market: the investment management firms that serve them.

Investment firms operate in a financial and regulatory environment that is constantly in flux. This unsteady state brings, to borrow the industry's true if overused refrain, challenges and opportunities. But to help clients take advantage of the latter, firms need to respond to the former. And they face many.

Between gyrating markets and evolving regulations, the investment landscape is always shifting the boundary of possibilities that defines the space in which firms operate. This boundary can move rapidly or turn unclear in periods of uncertainty, as when newly proposed regulations are pending but have yet to be ironed out or take effect, or when markets are unusually choppy.

One extreme instance was the collapse of Lehman Brothers, the storied financial services firm, in September 2008. In the days following, markets tumbled in mayhem and investors faced pandemonium. To contain the carnage and strengthen investor confidence, the U.S. Securities and Exchange Commission, in concert with the U.K. Financial Services Authority, took emergency action, temporarily banning the short-selling of financial-company stocks.[2] One could only imagine how restraining that prohibition was for hedge funds, which are founded on the very idea of being able to express negative views on any security through short positions.

To get a sense of the challenging pathways investment firms face, imagine having to write a composition on a chalkboard that has been erased only partially from earlier writing—and there you have it: the kind of messy canvas on which firms often need to chart a path for their clients.

In response to changing markets and regulations, investment managers may find themselves having to modify their products, alter their strategies or revise shareholder terms and conditions, and communicate those changes to clients. If the change represents a favorable development from the investor's point of view, there's clearly nothing to worry about with regard to client retention. But some changes introduce setbacks and would be less than welcome by the investor.

In such cases, maintain the following in your communication:

- **Be straightforward and sincere.**

  Straightforwardness and sincerity are self-evident musts: Investment managers owe their clients clarity and candor with respect to where their money stands and how any change in management may affect it. Yet they also owe it to themselves. Being frank about what led them to change their offering and what the implications are—even if that change may not win them a client—will at least fortify one of their most important assets: their reputation. The manager's integrity isn't just a universally prized virtue among investors, but also an expected one.

- **Be tactful and diplomatic.**

  Like any other business involving people's money, investing is a sensitive affair (more in Chapter 4 on communication style). It requires skillful handling so as not to arouse hostility or provoke resentment. Your word choices and overall tone should always be respectful, considerate, courteous, and conciliatory—rather than defensive, harsh, or confrontational—especially when broaching uncomfortable subjects.

- **Make the investor—not the firm you represent—your focus.**

  Put the investor at the center of your communication and its spotlight. Explain how you considered investors' needs, concerns, and objectives in the rationale behind making the change. Will it potentially benefit them in the long run despite short-term sacrifices? Is it the best, the most optimal, the least undesirable, or perhaps the only alternative to offer investors given the new circumstances that led to this change in the first place? And most important of all: How will the change enable *you* to better serve *them*? You may then base your reassurance on any of these factors.

One real-life example demonstrating a practical application of these guidelines involves a fund that invested in hedge funds, also known as a "fund of funds." But first, here is a brief background:

Some hedge funds, and funds that invest in them, have provisions that limit when and how much money investors can withdraw from a fund. Why do these provisions exist? Because withdrawals force funds to liquidate their positions in order to meet redemption requests and could strain the operation of a fund. These provisions mainly aim to protect funds that invest in illiquid securities (i.e., securities that cannot be easily sold or exchanged for cash without a substantial loss in value[3]), or that pursue highly complex, time-sensitive investment strategies (such as through the use of derivatives) to which inopportune withdrawals could be disruptive.

The market environment of 2008 and 2009 proved tumultuous beyond anything imaginable for hedge funds. Investors sold assets at fire-sale prices, and market liquidity dried up. As a result, one fund of funds, which had previously offered investors the ability to redeem its shares once a month, decided to limit the frequency of withdrawals to once every quarter-year, and had to notify its shareholders of the change. Consider the way it might have addressed its investors:

> *Subject: Change in Liquidity Terms*
> *Dear [INVESTOR]:*
> *In this period of unprecedented turbulence in the financial markets, we are doing everything we can to navigate a volatile climate in pursuit of attractive opportunities for returns on your investment with us.*
>
> *Given present liquidity levels among the hedge funds in which we invest, we have concluded that it would not be possible for us to maintain operational efficiency and deliver competitive performance without a modification to your fund's redemption provisions. As a result of this modification, we will no longer be able to offer Class A shares featuring monthly redemptions, beginning [MONTH/DAY].*
>
> *In lieu of your investment in Class A shares, you may elect to remain invested with the fund under the same fee terms through Class B shares, which offer quarterly redemptions. To do so, you would need to submit a request to transfer your current balance*

from Class A shares to Class B shares using the form included in this letter, which you would need to fill out and mail to our Investor Relations department by [MONTH/DAY]. Should you not submit a transfer request by this date, your investment will be automatically redeemed, and your redemption will be satisfied in cash.

We regret any inconvenience this change may cause you and would welcome your election to remain invested with us. In our view, the dislocation in the capital markets and newly consolidated hedge-fund industry present an investment opportunity. With redemptions limited to a quarterly basis, we believe your fund will be better positioned to capitalize on this opportunity and administer your investment in the most pragmatic fashion in the current environment.

If you have any questions or concerns, please do not hesitate to contact us at [CONTACT INFORMATION].

Thank you for your investment and confidence in [FIRM'S NAME].

Sincerely,

[NAME AND TITLE]

OTHER CONSIDERATIONS FOR REASSURING INVESTORS

What do we expect of our leaders in an hour of challenge? It's an instructive question writers can ask themselves as they pen reassurances to investors. Investment managers are their clients' leaders—perhaps not in a political sense, but certainly a financial one. They govern and administer portfolios and make decisions that affect investors' future.

The answer to the leadership question can thus provide a useful signpost: We expect of our leaders, among other things, to be confident; to take full interest in—and have thorough knowledge of—the details of what's going on; to possess good judgment and levelheadedness; to be present and visible as needed for providing counsel, giving direction and guiding the way; to take responsibility for their actions; and to assume accountability for results.

Apply the following five leadership qualities when reassuring your investors while pointing out why your firm believes it's the suitable one to lead them:

1. Assure investors of your continuing communication.

Communicating with regularity to apprise investors during difficult times is essential. Yet even if there's nothing new to report, continuous communication can be reassuring. Don't hesitate to express that idea in words, as in the following:

> *Market conditions may change—but what will not change is our belief in the importance of being in touch with you on a constant basis, no matter the environment. As a client of our firm, you can count on us to explore, analyze, and assess the range of issues affecting your portfolio, to help you make sense of them, and to guide you in making informed decisions.*

2. Maintain a levelheaded tone.

The calm, composure, and resourcefulness we expect of leaders sets the tone in which you communicate to investors. What does this mean from the practical standpoint of a writer? Providing investors with all the information they need to know, addressing their concerns candidly and, if possible, offering solutions without unduly alarming them.

To be sure, the world is not in want of woes, and one could easily unearth a frightening prospect at every turn. But if alarm is the very baseline of one's mindset, why stake out a monetary position in the capital markets in the first place and expose oneself to all its attendant risks? In taking such a position, investors knowingly assume the calculus of weighing potential gains against the risks of a loss (which, incidentally, you also need to disclose to them—prominently and unambiguously). And what they seek is the responsible, confident, and steady hand of someone who can help manage their stakes with rationality and equanimity.

Write for the investor in that spirit. It doesn't mean you should ever understate a risk, gloss it over with Pollyannaish views, lead investors on with a false sense of security, or misrepresent a problem. But it *does* mean you should give them a perspective that is levelheaded as much as it is realistic.

Here's a hypothetical example as an illustration of this concept. Suppose a high-category hurricane—we'll call her Hurricane Heather—afflicted a vast, populous area in the southern United States, with economic consequences for the entire country. Given the exposure of its portfolio to the U.S. market, a particular firm decided to issue special commentary to clients in order to explain the ramifications of this hurricane for investors. It could choose to open in the following manner:

> *Hurricane Heather appears to be one of the most destructive natural disasters in U.S. history. Our portfolio managers are greatly disturbed and worried by the tragedy it has left in*

its wake, which continues to unfold. Given this hurricane's far-reaching magnitude, we deeply fear that Heather might have a spillover effect on the national economy from coast to coast. In this special commentary, we provide you with our detailed perspective and investment outlook.

There's nothing inaccurate or inappropriate about such an opening, though its overall tone is tinged with apprehension that serves no apparent purpose, apart from expressing emotion. (There's a more appropriate opportunity—and perhaps a more effective way—to do that, which I'll get to shortly.)

Consider a more composed alternative for an opening that is no less accurate, fair, or informative, without underplaying the dimensions of the tragedy or showing indifference to others' misfortune:

Hurricane Heather is regarded by many as one of the most destructive natural disasters in U.S. history. Although historically, the financial markets in the United States have recovered quickly from natural disasters, the magnitude and effects of Heather, given what we know in its aftermath, may prove different. Our analysts believe this hurricane may have broader, long-term implications for the economy. In our continuing effort to keep investors informed, we provide you with the following perspective.

Your commentary could later end on a note of compassion:

Finally, in the wake of such devastation, we acknowledge the human toll as the foremost consequence of this disaster. The firm and its employees wish to express deep sorrow in the aftermath—and our heartfelt thoughts go out to all those who have been affected.

We hope this perspective provides you with useful insights for investment considerations.

3. Highlight your distinguishing characteristics.

Sources of reassurance for your investors are often closer to home than you might realize. This is the time to draw on your reservoir of distinction and highlight the unique reasons for why investors should maintain their confidence in you. (For more on how to articulate your distinguishing characteristics, see Chapter 5, Part 1.)

Some investment teams, for example, invest in their own strategies alongside clients of the firm, thus demonstrating genuine belief in their prospects of success and commitment to making it happen. Some structure their compensation to reflect the performance of their strategies, thereby ensuring close alignment with investors' interests. And some have relationships with, and privileged access to, government officials and corporate executives that enable them to perform original research and gain exclusive insights. These are just a few examples of differentiating features you may highlight in your reassurances, aside from your firm's talent pool, experience, capabilities, and long-term outlook.

4. **Offer a broadly gauged view of your performance—and hold yourself accountable for results.**

A track record of solid investment gains—especially if they exceed those of peer competitors—is a reassuring accomplishment that speaks for itself. Yet even if performance is lackluster, there might be a deeper story within the numbers that would support a reassuring narrative.

The concept of *upside* has more than one interpretation. In an absolute sense, it is the sheer percentage increase in the value of an investment. But from another point of view, there's also upside to having less downside, or at least affording investors a smoother ride from point A to point B with fewer shocks along the way, even if the overall gain for the entire period of the investment is more modest. Some investors—private and institutional—wish to build lasting wealth or manage their liabilities by reducing the amplitude of their portfolio's fluctuations. Rather than investing aggressively, they might prefer a disciplined, consistent effort to reduce potential losses and avoid taking on excessive risks, no matter how seductive the return prospects are. Indeed, for them, steadier performance can be reassuring despite the caveat of giving up some gains.

There would also be cause for reassurance if your performance were less negative than that of your peers, or than what would have been expected of you during a market downturn.

Then again, if your performance is poor with no particular justification or silver lining, do what investors expect of you as a leader: Take responsibility—and express your commitment to try to improve it, with the assumption that you can back your pledge with action, as in the following example:

> At InvestorPro, we realize that we have fallen short of meeting our clients' performance expectations this past year, but we will strive to do better the next.

Whenever appropriate, you may also explain what specific measures you are taking to address performance issues and attempt to improve future outcomes. Many investors will appreciate a forthright admission of your lack of success, an acknowledgment of their disappointment in the results, and a demonstration of how serious you are about course correction. "Honest marketing" is another way of looking at it.

5. **Avoid reflexive reassurances.**

Lastly, in responding to reassure investors, don't be reflexive, for it may show in your message, and you'd certainly not want to come off as disingenuous, unconvincing, or overly defensive. Rather than indiscriminately dumping onto your copy any conceivable reason you could find to assuage concerns or fend off criticism, be selective. Muster only the most pertinent arguments.

Authentic reassurance calls for organizational introspection, deep analysis, and deliberative writing. And if it is grounded in facts, it stands a good chance of winning investors' continued confidence.

NOTES

1. The National Association of Insurance Commissioners (NAIC) and the Center for Insurance Policy and Research.
2. www.sec.gov/news/press/2008/2008-211.htm. Retrieved on April 29, 2017.
3. Investopedia, LLC.

CHAPTER 3

Writing for Intermediaries

Some investors are self-sufficient. But many—both private and institutional—seek the guidance and counsel of intermediaries, by which I mean advisors and consultants, to navigate a broadening and increasingly elaborate universe of investment options.

Who are these intermediaries? In the United States, for example, they span three categories:

1. Financial advisors, who serve individuals on behalf of such institutions as wealth management firms, private banks, and broker/dealers
2. Registered investment advisors, or RIAs, who serve individuals independently and run their own practice, or who are part of an independent practice
3. Institutional investor consultants, who advise government and corporate sponsors of employee retirement plans, endowments, foundations, insurance companies, sovereign wealth funds, and others

The role of intermediaries is to help investors achieve their objectives. As facilitators, they help their clients formulate investment strategies, allocate money to appropriate assets, and manage risks. As gatekeepers, they evaluate investment management firms to tap for their client, cull funds on offer in the marketplace and vet them for quality, and maintain lists of recommended managers on the basis of track records and the clarity with which those managers convey the attributes and potential risks of their funds. Many advisors and consultants also act as fiduciaries and may make investments on their clients' behalf.

Investment writing serves investment firms in the strategic purpose of cultivating relationships with the intermediary community—and winning the endorsement of its members.

HOW INTERMEDIARIES EXPECT YOU TO COMMUNICATE

Communication is half the battle toward securing an intermediary's recommendation. Of course, an investment firm must also meet a host of essential criteria that are beyond the writer's ability to provide, such as the possession of certain technical skills, resources, or specialized capabilities; a history of competitive investment performance, favorable ratings from external agencies, retention of key personnel, and organizational stability; attractive fees; a demonstrable discipline of risk management; an investment philosophy that has been practiced consistently over time; assets under management in excess of a minimum threshold; sound operational infrastructure; quality client service; and a strong, reputable brand.

But these criteria, though necessary, are insufficient. An investment firm cannot win over advisors and consultants without communicating to them regularly, clearly, and comprehensively to include all the information they require to make a thorough evaluation. That's where writers come in. Here are some guidelines to keep in mind.

Communicate on a Consistent Basis

Make a point of updating intermediaries about your firm and its business—preferably at regularly scheduled intervals so as to afford them a predictable, reliable drumbeat of briefings. The frequency could be weekly, monthly, or quarterly—whatever you see fit given your volume of updates, the intermediary's needs, and the nature of your particular relationship.

Consider announcements about any combination of the following:

- *Firm news,* including key hires, management changes, and any other organizational updates of interest
- *Product news,* including the introduction of new funds, strategies, or vehicles; changes to existing funds, strategies, or investment personnel; updates on current matters affecting a firm's offerings, such as market events or new regulations; calendric milestones such as close dates of private funds; commentary on your investment performance; and other product-related affairs
- *A roundup of recently published investment literature* by your firm, including timely articles—or links to them—about topical issues of interest to investors and consultants, long-form research papers, case studies, capability brochures, blogs, infographics, and product profiles
- *A calendar of upcoming events and broadcasts* such as client webinars, webcasts, podcasts, and conferences—whether those your firm will host or those in which it will participate

Here's one example of what the opening summary of a newsletter for institutional investor consultants (which can also be formatted as a series of bullets for those who prefer that typographical approach) could look like:

Welcome to the first-quarter edition of the InvestorPro newsletter for institutional investor consultants. In this issue, we highlight our latest management updates, including the hiring of a chief economist, as well as the launch of a new infrastructure fund.

Our new podcast on the implications of Europe's monetary policy for fixed income is now available at [LINK]. We invite you to read our most recent literature, which includes a paper on positioning portfolios for prolonged volatility.

Finally, please save the date for an upcoming webinar on global asset allocation in today's environment, scheduled for [DATE]. This webinar will feature the head of our Multi-Asset Group, [NAME].

Crystallize the Details of Your Firm's Offerings

Toward their rigorous assessment of your firm, intermediaries demand a lucid, precise, and inclusive articulation of all the foundational elements of your firm's investment strategies, capabilities, and investment teams. They expect you to verbalize a cogent investment philosophy undergirding each strategy. They seek to understand the *modus operandi* your managers follow for identifying opportunities, evaluating them, making investment decisions, and running portfolios. They want a clear and visible account of your holdings and performance to validate your investment philosophy and process. And they require other such information as your risk-management practices, portfolio turnover, staff turnover, fund capacity, personnel skill sets, organizational infrastructure, and more.

Naturally, they also expect to learn about your firm's performance history. All the same, they understand that financial markets run in cycles—and that no one investment strategy can be designed to perpetually outperform all others. For this reason, they place a premium on the transparency and timeliness of your communications on all matters—not just your track record. The value of strong intermediary communications cannot be overstated.

For detailed guidance on articulating investment capabilities and strategies, refer to Chapter 5, Part 1.

Provide Timely, Turnkey Investment Literature

Approach your intermediary relationship as a partnership. Yes, advisors and consultants seek specific information from you to evaluate your firm for their clients—but they also expect your continuing support. As the mouthpiece of an investment firm that develops and manages strategies, conducts research, and offers analysis, you are in a position to aid their practice. By providing intermediaries with insightful literature that they and their clients can use to stay informed, you facilitate, shape, and enrich their dialogue with investors. You help them deliver more productive counsel. You also contribute to their arsenal of tools for client prospecting, outreach, and retention.

Offer them turnkey investment content—the kind that's packaged for immediate use, that they can efficiently consume and readily share with investors without having to do extra research or legwork. (Refer to Chapter 5 for more on forms of investment literature.)

It's okay to provide literature that has a long shelf life—but make sure to also include content that's timely and topical. The intermediary business, much like investment management, is event-driven. Advisors and consultants find such content useful for client engagements in response to market developments as they try to figure out how a given event may affect their clients' portfolios—and how their clients should respond. Conversely, timely and topical content could plant the seed of outreach in their heads, galvanize them to contact their clients in short order, and use your literature as the basis of a discussion.

When appropriate, make your literature prescriptive by offering investment recommendations or solutions that they can relay to their clients or use in their consultations. What specifically do intermediaries look for? It varies.

Advisors of private clients focus on household financial planning and wealth management. They develop strategies to allocate money between different asset classes (such as stocks and bonds) that help individuals reach their financial objectives. These advisors favor opportune pointers. For example, if your firm finds that market fundamentals bode well for technology, energy, and consumer-staples stocks, you can offer them an investment perspective on "three stock sectors that may be poised for growth." A dislocation in the senior loan market, as another example, could warrant a paper on "why the time may be right to invest in senior loans with attractive risk/return characteristics."

The topics you cover should resonate with advisors and their clients (see Part 2 of Chapter 5 for examples)—and your story angles need to be incisive. Suppose, for instance, that country X enacted a fiscal stimulus plan that bodes well for its financial markets. A feature on "how X's fiscal stimulus plan could reignite markets" could be good, but one on "an investment strategy to consider on the heels of X's stimulus plan" could be even better. Don't hold back on sharing perspectives that go against the consensus, assuming you have solid arguments to back them up. Contrarian opinions actually have a greater chance of standing out in the advisor's inbox and getting read.

Consultants of institutional investors can benefit from similar content. Yet they also require more sophisticated literature that provides technical solutions to the complex challenges their clients' portfolios face in the short, medium, and long term. For instance, they may take interest in a paper on portfolio-overlay strategies for managing currency exposure, or interest in, say, a beta-management strategy for multi-asset-class portfolios aimed at curbing risk imbalances and improving capital efficiency.

As an aside, there are also consultants who provide counsel to sponsors of defined-contribution retirement plans, which are a type of plan in which the employer, employee, or both make contributions on a regular basis, such as 401(k) plans in the United States. Unlike sponsors of defined-benefit retirement plans (mentioned in the list of institutional investors in Chapter 2), sponsors of defined-contribution plans aren't actual investors. However, as employers, they have a fiduciary responsibility to evaluate and construct the most suitable retirement plans for their employees—and they tap consultants to help them accomplish this objective. Investment firms communicate to those consultants in an effort to get their funds evaluated for inclusion in plan menus.

Like their brethren who serve private and institutional investors, consultants of defined-contribution plan sponsors can benefit from instructive literature to use with their clients. For example, the growing popularity of low-cost, exchange-traded funds (ETFs) prompted one firm to publish a paper for consultants on how sponsors can reconfigure the fund lineups of their plans to incorporate ETFs, lower plan costs, and offer employees a rounded selection of options.

Keep Your Communications Targeted

Sure, intermediaries expect a detailed account of everything they need to know—but no more. Between managing investments and client relationships, prospecting for new clients and growing their practice, setting aside the time for meetings and phone calls, and the administrative day-to-day chores entailed in running their business, advisors are time-starved, as are institutional investor consultants. To open the floodgates of information and inundate them would be worse than a breach of good taste; it could actually jeopardize your firm's intermediary relationships. (E-mail overload, for instance, can be anathema to them.)

Communicate comprehensively—but keep your writing focused and your communications selective. Ensure that they are of immediate relevance to the needs of advisors' clients. For example, rather than offering advisors a paper on how inflation is affected by central-bank policies and why it may pick up, you may consider a more targeted paper explaining what the prospect of inflation means for investors' portfolios—and what anticipatory strategies they could pursue. Likewise, consider supplementing market commentary and prognostications with your views on investment strategies to consider in light of your outlook.

As earlier mentioned, the content needs of institutional investor consultants are broader and more complex than those of private-client advisors. But they, too, require a focus on the current, the pertinent, and the practical.

Many advisors and consultants seek managers who offer strategies that complement their menu of offerings or fall neatly into specific categories of investment objectives (such as inflation protection, growth, or volatility mitigation) that dovetail with, or fit into, the investment model they envision for their clients. There may also be products—especially of a new and unfamiliar type—that advisors don't even know they can't live without. If that's the case, lead them to the foregoing conclusion.

INTERMEDIARIES DON'T HAVE IT EASY, SO HELP THEM OUT

Intermediaries face a progressively more complex, competitive, and fast-paced industry. Markets gyrate. Investment offerings evolve. Pressing issues that affect investors' portfolios emerge frequently. Clients have lofty expectations, and they expect advisors to gain a holistic view of their multifarious needs. Advisory practices must adapt to changes quickly in order to continue delivering productive counsel and quality service.

In a writer's capacity, your role is to help advisors evaluate your firm, but also to help them help their clients—and position them to be the most informed people in the room. You can do so by providing them with the buy-side perspective of your firm on the financial markets; by explaining the issues affecting investors' portfolios; by arming them with suitable strategies and solutions for their clients to consider; and by broadening their knowledge about investment and financial affairs on a product-agnostic basis.

CHAPTER 4

Stylistic Considerations for Investment Writing

"It's not that I'm a slave to style; I just have tremendous respect for it."

—Bruce Felton

My quoted friend, a talented writer and erstwhile colleague, is onto something. I'll take the second half of his thought—the respect for style—a bit further as it relates to the subject of this book.

Memo to all investment writers: Content may be king—but style never goes out of style. By *style* I mean:

- The vocabulary and tone of language that reflect the company's or author's distinct voice and character.
- A deliberate manner of writing intended to clarify or refine a message, make it accessible, and engage investors in a particular way. (Clarity ensures that investors unequivocally understand what you're saying. Accessibility ensures they're able to absorb it efficiently, without undue effort. And to engage investors—whether by getting them to take action or simply be interested in what you're saying—you need to command their attention.)

When it comes to investment writing, style boils down to more than just form or appearance. It's an essential instrument for conveying and differentiating the image of an investment firm or professional, communicating to investors effectively, and forging relationships with them.

Relationship is the operative word, for investing is both transactional *and* personal: It is a financial affair, but also a private affair, between investor and manager. On what basis does the former pick the latter?

A manager's credentials—her public reputation, performance track record, industry awards, and other bona fides—are clearly considered. Yet the investor seeks more than the qualifications exhibited on paper. After all, there's no shortage of skilled managers from whom to choose. Among them, investors will need to single out the one or two or handful of managers they would deem especially qualified to serve as caretakers of their assets. And they will handpick those with whom they feel they can build rapport: a relationship of trust and confidence, of understanding and comfort, and of mutual regard.

Your writing style is the gateway to such rapport—one that will set the tenor of the investor/manager relationship, through communication, at the touchpoint of introduction and beyond.

Here's the challenge: Though style is often described in general terms, the ability to capture a particular style in writing—to strike that characteristic tone claimed as the voice of a firm or investment professional—can be elusive. Why? Because style is nebulous and wide-ranging. It can take on countless shades. You may be able to distinguish between different styles once you see them, but calibrating your tone for nuance and navigating word subtleties are a gingerly craft that requires a great deal of discretion.

Remember that investors' finances are at stake—as is your reputation—and they deserve utmost respect and sensitivity from the managers to whom they assign such weighty responsibility. Even small stylistic choices can greatly affect how investors perceive you and your message and decide whether to entrust you with their money. Apply the same judiciousness to those choices as your target audience would apply in assessing the firm or investment professional you represent in your writing.

That's not to say you should constrain your writing style to a straightjacket of stuffy conformism. By all means, take creative license. Make your content absorbing, engaging, and all-around worthwhile for the investor to read. Write with flair and originality. Be provocative and thought provoking. Spice up your narrative literature—such as investment commentary or research papers—with anecdotes so long as they are context-appropriate, relate to a topic of interest to investors, and aren't too lengthy or digressive. For certain communications, your style may range from formal to conversational. You can even be, in tasteful measure, ironic and humorous. In his monthly commentary, one author invoked a horror scene from Steven Spielberg's 1975 classic, *Jaws*, to describe the predicament of central bankers in dealing with the repercussions of the financial crisis of 2008. Bracketed by plenty of useful analysis, his analogy was imaginative, on point, and appropriately brief.

This brings me to the following caveat: In whatever way you choose to be creative, stay focused and informative, show respect for your readers' time, and don't be flippant. Investing is serious business. Another author left some commentators scratching their heads when, in an issue of his periodical and widely circulated investment outlook, he opened with a eulogy for his cat, which had died a week earlier. Granted, his eulogy was heartfelt and part of a larger point he tried to make about the ephemerality of life. And perhaps it was a liberty he could afford to take given his renown and established credibility in the investor community. But unless you have an exceptional relationship with your investors that grants you such broad latitude for personal expression, I would not recommend investment literature as a place for random philosophical musings—much less for lamentations on the demise of a feline pet—that aren't instructive from an investor's point of view, or that risk appearing irreverent and unserious.

Even when being conversational—the most natural way to address your investors as fellow humans—you're bound by a business partnership that requires a slightly elevated level of formality in your dialogue. A relaxed tone is acceptable; slangy is not.

When determining your writing style, also keep in mind that regulatory authorities will vet your every word. There's more on the legal aspects of investment writing to consider in Chapter 7.

SETTING THE APPROPRIATE STYLE

Your choice of style ought to reflect the following triad of considerations:

1. The desired image and voice an investment firm or professional wishes to project
2. The type of literature being written
3. The investor's presumed knowledge about the subject matter

I stress *triad* because these considerations go hand in hand, ergo none of them should be weighed in isolation without regard to the two others. As an example of their interconnectedness, consider the obvious: You can author a superbly written, thoroughly researched paper on a complex topic using technical terminology to convey your ideas—but the paper will accomplish nothing if the investor's knowledge is insufficient to understand it. As another example, some types of investor communications, such as a letter to shareholders from a portfolio manager, or an instructive video, can strike a more personal and conversational tone than, say, a research paper or a firm-authored brochure outlining investment capabilities.

Let's take a closer look at how you weigh these three considerations when setting the most appropriate writing style.

The Desired Image and Voice an Investment Firm or Professional Wishes to Project

Many investment firms have formalized style guides that provide writers with general pointers regarding firm-specific tone and language. But no style manual, however comprehensive, can cover all the possibilities in terms of word choice, sentence structure, or overall flow. For all those, judgment calls are required.

How does a writer make them? Experience and intuition can help. Over time, a writer can become sufficiently familiar with a firm or individual author—be it a portfolio manager, analyst, economist, or chief investment officer—to divine what sounds, looks, and feels suitable, and what doesn't. Do the words reflect their vocabulary, culture, and tradition? Are they in line with what the firm's clients have come to expect? As writers acquire industry knowledge, expand their investment vocabulary, and learn about their audiences, they will be able to refine their stylistic choices in ways that best suit those audiences.

It also helps to anthropomorphize the firm you represent. If you had to think of your firm in human terms, how would you describe its personality? In what manner, by extension, would you envision it speaking to its audience? And what's the audience in question?

To demonstrate this exercise, picture two hypothetical investment firms: One is professorial in character; the other can be personified as a savvy advisor. The professorial firm's literature reflects a formal, expositional style characterized by heavier use of technical language and an erudite tone you'd associate with academic journals. That style is fitting, because the firm caters to highly sophisticated investors, has sizable research divisions, employs legions of analysts, and seeks to share with clients the product of its resources.

In contrast, the savvy-advisor firm caters to the more basic investor. It aspires to be perceived as a partner you can call up anytime for a quick chat or brief consultation—perhaps to request a clear explanation of a complex topic. In its investment literature, this firm favors a simple, matter-of-fact style over an expositional one. It frequently makes use of bulleted lists and highlighted sidebars for at-a-glance reading. Its vocabulary is common, a bit more casual and breezy, and warmer than a formal institutional voice. And its explanations are elementary as they enlist explanatory substitutes for technical terms and industry vernacular.

Imagine how both firms might convey the same message in very different styles:

Example #1

Professorial firm: We believe equity valuations are high.

Savvy-advisor firm: We think stocks are expensive.

Example #2

> **Professorial firm:** Exchange-traded funds have democratized access to an array of asset classes historically available only to select investors. Further, they introduce an economical alternative to mutual funds, providing comparable diversification as cost-advantaged vehicles.
>
> **Savvy-advisor firm:** Exchange-traded funds can:
> - Provide exposure to many different types of assets, including some that were once out of reach for certain investors; and
> - Offer a low-cost alternative to mutual funds for diversifying your portfolio.

Example #3

> **Professorial firm:** Investors are more defensive this year than 12 months ago, and we're observing a flight to quality, as our research indicates in Exhibit 1.
>
> **Savvy-advisor firm:** Investors are being more cautious this year than last, and we're seeing a shift toward lower-risk assets, as you can see in the illustration below.

Example #4

> **Professorial firm:** Asian markets may test new lows as ripples from China's economic slowdown continue to spread.
>
> **Savvy-advisor firm:** Asian markets may head even lower and reach a series of bottoms as China's economic slowdown continues to affect the region.

Example #5

> **Professorial firm:** For inquiries, please contact your account representative listed below.
>
> **Savvy-advisor firm:** Have a question? We're happy to help: Simply email your account representative listed below.

This is not to suggest one style is better. Both can be effective, depending on the type of firm and investor in question and on the nature of the firm/investor relationship. But the differences between them illustrate the sort of careful stylistic calls that investment writers need to make every day.

The Type of Literature Being Written

Style cannot be removed from context and objective. The communication vehicle chosen to convey *what* you say should also affect *how* you're saying it by virtue of the purpose your vehicle serves.

No stylistic rule can be set in stone, but here are some examples, suggestions, and general considerations:

- *Research papers* showcase investigative knowledge and serve to educate and inform. Since they tend to be more analytically rigorous and technically dense than other types of literature, they are written with gravitas—an air of seriousness and scholarliness that dignifies their intellectual heft. And if they are to be taken credibly, they should not be written promotionally (more on why in Part 2 of Chapter 5).
- *Brochures* serve to advertise investment products and capabilities explicitly and can take on a promotional style. They tend to be more conversational and personal than research papers, such as by addressing readers directly in the second person (e.g., *you* or *your*), especially if written for individual investors rather than institutions. Many brochures seek reader engagement through a call to action, such as an appeal to visit a website or contact a firm representative.
- *Investment commentary and personal letters to the investor* that are authored, bylined, and signed by an individual (such as a portfolio manager or chief investment officer) can take on the author's personal style. Some authors are expressively heartfelt. Some are informal. Some are conspicuously unpretentious—shall we say downright folksy?—while still managing to be authoritative and serious by writing substantively and respectfully.
- *Firm-authored commentary on investment performance* (such as periodical performance reports of investment funds) and *firm-authored letters to investors* on official matters are written formally as befitting any communication issued by an institutional source.
- *Investment proposals (RFP responses)* strike a formal tone, because they are official documents put forward for consideration as the basis of an agreement between the investor and the investment manager. They can and should be written as a pitch to acquire a prospect's business. Proposals are typically responses to institutional solicitations, cater to more advanced readers, and may employ heavily technical vocabulary. (There's more on recommended practices for writing RFP responses in Part 1 of Chapter 5.)
- *Video scripts* are written for voiceovers or as scripts to be read by an investment professional, often from a teleprompter, for on-camera appearances. Since formality in speech can sound stilted and unnatural, these scripts should be written conversationally to suit the oral nature of the video medium.
- *Presentations* are typically displayed to an audience as a series of slides (whether in PowerPoint or an equivalent application) on an investment

product or topic. They should be written in the most condensed, economical way possible because (1) slides have very little space for copy; (2) they are merely a visual accompaniment to the presenter, who takes center stage; and (3) the audience, whose attention is divided between the presenter and the presentation, has limited absorption capacity and can only handle tidbits of text rather than lengthy prose.

Consider writing your slides in a telegraphic format: Use bullet points that encapsulate key messages while omitting nonessential words, such as certain modal and auxiliary verbs, prepositions, conjunctions, and descriptors. Hence, the following sentence...

So far, despite multiple events that have occurred over the past several weeks, our outlook for the Eurozone's economy remains unchanged.

...may become the following bullet point in a presentation:

■ *Outlook for Eurozone economy: unchanged*

To demonstrate these stylistic differences, consider a host of passages for different communication vehicles on bond-related topics and funds:

Type of Literature	Passage
Research paper	With yields near historic lows and interest rates poised to rise, Treasuries and investment-grade bonds—typically perceived as having lower risk—could lose ground. The bond market's vulnerability to rising rates may result in price declines that pose a risk to any investor in fixed income. However, our research suggests that in the current environment, bonds with less-than-perfect credit quality may provide investors with three important benefits when compared with their investment-grade counterparts: 1. Lower interest-rate sensitivity; 2. An attractive income component that could drive higher total returns; and 3. A significant spread over higher-grade alternatives, even on a risk-adjusted basis.

Type of Literature	Passage
Brochure	We provide an array of fixed-income strategies—from investment-grade to high-yield—that cover a range of bond maturities. Whatever your time horizon or risk tolerance, our investment professionals are dedicated to providing options to suit your financial objectives. For more information, visit our website at [COMPANY WEBSITE].
A personal letter to investors from a portfolio manager	Dear Shareholder: It was a rollercoaster year for bond investors, but my team and I have made an effort to shield your fund from some of the turbulence by trimming positions in sectors that struggled in this challenging economic climate, such as luxury-goods manufacturers. Yet despite the rough ride of the past 12 months, we're more optimistic about the year ahead, and here's why...
A firm-authored letter to investors	Dear Shareholder: We are writing to inform you that the Special Meeting of Shareholders for the InvestorPro Global Bond fund held on [DATE] has been adjourned in order to permit further solicitation of votes on a proposal to approve the acquisition of your fund. As a reminder, the proposal put forward would allow for the acquisition of the assets and assumption of the liabilities of your fund by [COMPANY X] and the issuance of shares that have the same aggregate net asset value as the shares of your current fund immediately prior to your fund's acquisition.

Type of Literature	Passage
	Our records indicate that we have not received voting instructions for your account(s). In an effort to avoid any further expenses to the Fund, we are asking you to please take a moment now to submit your vote.
RFP response	InvestorPro High Yield is a fixed-income fund that seeks high income and capital appreciation by investing in bonds of moderate credit quality that we believe will provide attractive risk-adjusted returns. We focus on fundamental research of individual issuers in our investment process. Additionally, we aim to maximize returns by modulating our exposure to different tiers of credit ratings throughout the market cycle.
Video script for an educational segment on high-yield bonds	So, what is a high-yield bond? Essentially, it's a debt security, issued by a corporation, that offers a higher rate of interest because of its higher risk of default. But it's important to remember: Not all high-yield bonds are the same. Some have greater credit risk than others. Let's talk a little about how this risk is determined ...
Presentation slide	**Forecast for next year:** ■ Resilient bond market ■ Narrow credit spreads ■ Greater demand for high yield

The Investor's Presumed Knowledge about the Subject Matter

"Knowing your audience" is the first order of business when deciding how to word your investment literature. And although there's no prescriptive formula that can cover a boundless universe of writing options, it's helpful to distinguish between three broad categories of investors along the knowledge spectrum, as mentioned in Chapter 2:

1. The first category consists of mainstream retail investors who, for the most part, have only rudimentary—if any—knowledge about investing. Retail investors require simplified versions of technical material and explanatory substitutes for, or clarifications of, all but the most widely known investment terms (such as *stocks* and *bonds*).
2. The second category consists of investors with a moderate-to-advanced understanding of investment concepts, and they include high-net-worth investors, as well as private-client advisors, to whom you would also need to communicate (see Chapter 3). Not all wealthy individuals necessarily belong to this category. But plenty of them, as one would expect, have attained higher-than-average investment literacy through the complex financial management of their estates and businesses. Some might have become wealthy precisely *because* they are seasoned investors. And many meet the high minimum investment amounts required to access complex financial instruments (such as certain derivatives), products (such as hedge funds), and direct private investments (including private-equity, real-estate, and infrastructure funds) that may not be available to the general public. Therefore, literature intended for affluent investors may contain advanced material by virtue of their eligibility for more sophisticated offerings.
3. Institutional investors are usually, for manifest reasons, the most technically literate, as are the consultants who serve them. The amounts they invest are vast, their needs complex, and their access to the capital markets unlimited. Institutional literature typically takes on a more formal tone than its retail sibling. But never lose sight of the fact that institutional readers are also people, even if they happen to represent clients of organizational rather than personal nature. These readers—just like any other—need to be engaged and their interests piqued. So, while formality may be more appropriate, try to push creative boundaries beyond the prosaic (more on that later).

How should writers modulate their investment vocabulary to suit these three audiences? To what extent should they use technical language? Ah, the jargon question.

ON USING JARGON

Jargon is a controversial matter among communication practitioners. Some argue for minimizing its use or avoiding it altogether for the benefit of clearer communication. But jargon, by its foremost definition, is merely slang for something quite useful called nomenclature. If used appropriately, it should contribute to your writing rather than diminish clarity.

As a naming system of specialized terms, nomenclature exists in practically every branch of knowledge or line of work—investments included—for good reason. These terms may be technical and even esoteric, yet they are usually the most precise and economical way to describe certain things, especially if those things are intricate or complex. Many technical terms don't have one-word substitutes, and attempts at replacing them with more common language may lead to circumlocutions—the use of many words where fewer would do (though, of course, you're always better off using more words to describe a concept in a simpler manner for less knowledgeable investors).

Investment nomenclature, in particular, contains a body of pithy, incisive terms that can lend exactness, brevity, and professional authority to your copy. And yet, they are never to be used over the reader's head or at the expense of clarity—the *sine qua non* of this trade.

Here are eight guidelines to consider about using and explaining jargon:

1. Refrain from explaining certain jargon to highly sophisticated investors.
2. Distinguish between three broad levels of investment literacy.
3. Consider three alternatives to explaining jargon.
4. Cut through extraneous technical detail.
5. If you risk being vague, err on the side of clarity.
6. Introduce fresh alternatives to trite jargon.
7. Be discerning about nuances.
8. Always use plain language.

Refrain from Explaining Certain Jargon to Highly Sophisticated Investors

The use of certain technical vocabulary is practically *de rigueur* when addressing sophisticated investors who would be expected to know what it meant beyond a doubt. For example, it's safe to assume that any institutional investor would know what a "bid/ask spread" is without having to explain the concept. Moreover, an explanation wouldn't just be unnecessary, but also detractive. Take the following passage:

> *Bid/ask spreads of actively traded senior loans have widened significantly under market pressure over the past several weeks. However, today's spreads are merely a return to the approximate 5-year average.*

If, in this case, you interjected with an explanation of a bid/ask spread, or used an explanatory substitute (i.e., "the difference between the highest price that buyers are willing to pay for senior loans and the lowest price that sellers are willing to accept for them"), you'd find yourself needlessly lengthening your copy and belaboring your point. You might even risk coming across as off-key and out of touch with your audience or as lacking respect for its understanding of the subject matter.

Distinguish Between the Three Broad Levels of Investment Literacy

1. Retail (Mass-market) Investors When communicating to the general public, explain all but the most familiar terms. What qualifies as familiar? Any term considered common knowledge—the kind you could comfortably classify as household financial vocabulary.

In the Common Category (requiring no explanation):	In the Uncommon or Less Common Category (requiring explanation):
Interest rates	Interest-rate swap
Dividends	Dividend yields
Bonds/Stocks	Bond convexity
Securities	Securitization
Bond maturity	Duration
Inflation	Leverage

It would take a separate book to cover the full body of investment vocabulary, so those are just some examples. Also, there's no hard-and-fast rule for deciding which terms are sufficiently common by retail investors so as to obviate an explanation, and which aren't. It's up to the writer to apply common sense—pun intended—in each case. In some instances, a legal specialist at your firm might weigh in and require explanations of certain nomenclature to certify your literature as adequate for public consumption and compliant by regulatory standards.

As an aside, there's always an opportunity to define even the most basic investment terms—such as *stocks* or *bonds*—in separate educational literature, as explained in Part 3 of Chapter 5. But when penning non-educational literature for the retail investor, you can assume your audience has a baseline of common knowledge. The alternative may be impractical, as you could find yourself turning every little brochure into a veritable encyclopedia of financial entries.

2. Investors with Moderate Knowledge The situation is more ambiguous when it comes to explaining less-than-common nomenclature to investors of moderate knowledge. One may safely presume that institutional investors would know what *arbitrage, yield curves,* and *contango* mean, whereas many or most retail investors would require an explanation. But what about high-net-worth investors and their advisors? To some these terms may be familiar while to others not. In any case, if you're uncertain your entire reader audience would understand a technical term, pair it with an explanation.

3. Investors with Advanced Knowledge Do the most sophisticated investors know it all? Not necessarily.

The investment profession is broad and deep. It contains multiple specialized disciplines involving different asset classes, markets, transactions, and analytics. And each has some of its own exclusive nomenclature that is the province of a relatively narrow segment of investment practitioners.

As a rule of thumb, make a point of explaining esoteric terms in niche areas, as not all investors—even among the highly knowledgeable—may be familiar with them. Examples include:

- Private equity and debt (e.g., PIK toggle, weighted average cost of capital, bridge loans)
- Real estate (e.g., cap rates, class A properties)
- Uncommon investment vehicles (e.g., structured investment vehicles, or SIVs; and inverse ETFs)
- Uncommon financial instruments or monetary contracts, such as exotic derivatives (e.g., swaptions)
- Foreign exchange (e.g., floating exchange rate, spot rate)
- Wonkish terms in economics and finance, such as arcane statistics and indicators for describing the economic environment (e.g., the Purchasing Manager's Index, or PMI).

On the other hand, you may not need to explain terms that cut across investment disciplines or are generally more common, such as:

- Measures of investment performance (e.g., Sharpe ratio, alpha, tracking error, standard deviation)
- Financial metrics (e.g., internal rate of return, or IRR)
- Market and price behavior (e.g., risk-on/risk-off, mean reversion)
- Run-of-the-mill investment vehicles (e.g., '40 Act funds; exchange traded funds, or ETFs)
- Plain-vanilla financial instruments (e.g., forwards, futures, swaps, commercial paper)
- Investment strategies (e.g., sector rotation, synthetic exposure, overweight/underweight positions);
- Elementary terms in economics and finance (e.g., gross domestic product, or GDP; core inflation)

Again, when in doubt about your readers' familiarity with a term, opt for the conservative route and explain it.

Alternatives to Explaining Jargon

If you find yourself having to explain a potentially unfamiliar term, there are four ways to go about doing it:

1. **Introduce the term first and then open a successive sentence with an explanation.** This approach can accommodate long or complex explanations because it prefaces them with the term itself to lead the discussion. Here's one passage featuring an explanation of *PIK toggle*:

   > *Our analysis of the private equity market shows that many deals contain a feature called "pay-in-kind (PIK) toggle." This feature offers borrowers a series of choices on how to pay accrued interest in the first several years of a debt security. Using PIK toggle, borrowers could choose between paying interest in cash; paying interest entirely "in-kind" by adding it to the principal amount and, in effect, borrowing more money to pay interest on their existing debt; or paying half of the interest in cash and half of it in-kind.*

2. **Introduce the term first and then explain it in apposition in the same sentence.** This approach works better for shorter explanations. For example:

   > *We look at duration—a bond's price sensitivity to changes in interest rates—when evaluating in which bonds to invest.*

3. **Lead with the explanation and then cite the term as an afterthought.** This approach may also work well for a shorter, simpler explanation— one you could launch into straightaway without having to introduce the term for it first. The following passage, written circa 2007, explains what cap rates are in this manner:

   > *The Japanese real estate market lays claim to a number of advantages, one of which concerns the ratios between the cash flows that properties produce and their value. These ratios, known as cap rates, are critical indicators of real estate values. Japan is among the few countries in which property owners can attain positive arbitrage between cap rates and borrowing costs, using leverage to achieve higher income on their assets.*

4. **Relegate the explanation to a footnote, an endnote, or an entry in a glossary of terms at the end of your piece.** Use this approach if you would not want to impose an explanation of the term on your body copy—whether because the explanation is very long or inessential and would disrupt the flow of your piece, or because you suspect most readers would likely be familiar with the term, but would still like to incorporate an unobtrusive explanation for everyone's benefit.

Here's one example footnoting the definition of *correlation*:

> *As emerging asset classes, farmland and timberland may offer low or negative* correlations* *with traditional assets because they are relatively illiquid, infrequently traded, and insulated from commodity speculation, such as options trading.*

---

*Correlation *is a statistical measure of the co-movement between two variables (such as securities). The value of a correlation can range from −1 to +1. A positive correlation indicates that two given variables move in lockstep, whereas a negative correlation indicates that two variables move in opposite directions. A correlation of zero means that two given variables are independent of one another.*

Cut Through Extraneous Technical Detail

In certain situations, it may be prudent to get past particular technical details if they are beside your main point, and assuming you could find explanatory substitutes that are shorter or simplified.

Example 1:

> **Technical:** We recommend that investors reposition their fixed-income portfolio's following the U.S. Federal Reserve's decision yesterday to raise **the target for the overnight bank lending rate, also known as the federal funds rate.**

> **Simplified:** We recommend that investors reposition their fixed-income portfolio's following the U.S. Federal Reserve's decision yesterday to raise **interest rates.**

True, the verbose version contains a more precise description of what the Federal Reserve actually modifies in the arcane process of raising the interest rate. But unless your intent is to address elements or aspects of the process itself—or to specify what the exact interest rate is, which would require qualifying it as the federal funds rate—there's no value in adding such level of detail and risk detracting from the focus of your message, especially when communicating to a general audience. In this case, you might as well simplify your description and afford readers a logical shortcut to the larger, more important point you're trying to make about repositioning fixed-income portfolios for a rising-rate environment.

Example 2:

Technical: Managers of unconstrained long-only strategies have exhibited higher information ratios, which are the returns that a manager generates actively (or alpha) divided by their standard deviation.

Simplified: Managers of unconstrained long-only strategies have exhibited higher information ratios, which reflect their higher consistency in generating returns in excess of the broad market.

(In the simplified version, you can footnote the definition of "information ratio" for audiences that may not be familiar with the term.)

If You Risk Being Vague, Err on the Side of Clarity

Investment terms are usually explicit. But in common parlance, some are used interchangeably with others as a kind of vernacular that may introduce ambiguity and warrant clarification.

Example 1:

Take the use of *discount* in this instance:

*Against a backdrop of anemic economic growth, equity markets have **discounted** a potential wave of disappointing corporate earnings later in the year.*

A lay investor may think you meant to say that equity markets have assigned a lower probability to the prospect of disappointing corporate earnings. But actually, this is a vernacular way of saying that investors have lowered (or discounted) their return expectations from equities in anticipation of weaker corporate earnings later in the year, and that stock prices have come down to reflect those expectations.

Consider a clearer alternative:

*Equity markets are down, having **priced in** a potential wave of disappointing corporate earnings later this year amid anemic economic growth.*

Example 2:

> *Beta* is another example: In mathematical terms, it is a coefficient—a numerical measure that represents a security's or portfolio's sensitivity to market movements, as in the following:
>
> *The fund's portfolio has maintained a modest beta of 0.3 to the market index.*
>
> Yet *beta* is sometimes used as a byword for market returns, as opposed to returns generated by manager skill (or *alpha*, which itself has multiple definitions in the financial literature):
>
> *In this bull market, we're focused on generating beta for our investors.*
>
> Some would argue that using *beta* for anything other than its proper mathematical definition is a fallacy. (The S&P 500 Index could be up by, let's say, 15 percent. Yet for you to capture the full 15 percent return, your beta coefficient would need to be 1. Besides, beta can still be positive even if the market returned zero or declined. Nonetheless, given their linear association, the former has come to signify the latter.) Granted, the intended meaning of *beta* can usually be inferred from the context in which it is used. But for less-than-seasoned investors, you might want to include a clarification of how you're defining beta, or simply reserve the term for its precise numerical meaning.

Example 3:

> The investment area of fixed income also has its share of vernacular. For example, the word *rates* in certain contexts refers not to interest rates, but to government bonds and related securities, such as interest-rate swaps and options on those swaps, also known as interest-rate swaptions. (To write that "rates have rallied" is to mean that the prices of such securities have gone up.)
>
> As another example, the word *credit* in specific instances refers to the corporate—rather than government—sector of the bond market, and *credits* are simply corporate bonds.
>
> If you detect even the smallest possibility of being misconstrued, follow the conservatively explicit route and simply spell it out.

Example 4:

For investors of basic or moderate literacy, beware of using the kind of jargon that might confuse them into making the wrong logical deduction, as in the following:

We reduced our underweight position in X.

This is one of those instances in which two negatives create a positive: Reducing an underweight position in an investment actually means *adding* exposure to that investment by enlarging the position to one that is less underweight, or to one that is market weight. For those who may misconstrue it as an act of trimming the size of the position, you could crystalize the idea a bit further:

We upped our exposure to X from underweight to equal weight.

Or:

We upped our exposure to X and are now less underweight than we were before.

Example 5:

In certain contexts, avoid using words that can double for investment terms and create misinterpretations, as in the following:

When investing in X, we evaluate a number of options.

Does *options* in this instance mean "alternative courses of action"? Or is it a reference to options contracts, which are agreements that grant their purchasers the right to buy or sell an asset at a later date and an agreed-upon price? That's for you to clarify.

Introduce Fresh Alternatives to Trite Jargon

There's another meaning for jargon having nothing to do with language. According to the *New Oxford American Dictionary*, jargon can also be a type of translucent or colorless mineral. It's a literal definition, though also—ironically—a good metaphor for the kind of dull, overused jargon that betrays a lack of original thought.

A classic example is the common characterization of investment processes as either "top-down" (i.e., looking at broad economic or industry conditions in order to identify securities in which to invest) or "bottom-up" (i.e., focusing attention solely on the individual security when evaluating an investment opportunity). There are probably no better illustrative metaphors to describe how an investment process works, though they utterly lack distinction, as virtually all firms characterize their processes in the same way. And they've come to substitute for more meaningful descriptions of what portfolio managers do.

Take the following sentence, which is a slight variation of something that appeared in one firm's investment commentary:

The geographic diversity of our fund's portfolio is not the result of a top-down investment process, but rather the result of our bottom-up orientation.

Diane Gargiulo, founder and president of Gargiulo + Partners, suggests ways in which to make investor communications "just a little fresher, without alarming investors, the markets, your colleagues or yourself." Borrowing from how she addressed the "top-down" and "bottom-up" clichés, one might consider the following augmented alternative, which invests them with more substance and depth:

The geographic diversity of our fund's portfolio is not a deliberate result of regional selection based on analysis of countries' macroeconomic conditions. Rather, it is the incidental result of stock selection through analysis of specific companies and their business fundamentals.

As Gargiulo points out, some jargon is so entrenched as to make one overlook how stale common phrases are (e.g., "We perform a quantitative analysis of stocks")—and how they can easily be ditched in favor of fresher, more explanatory ones ("We seek to understand stock behavior by using sophisticated mathematical and statistical modeling").

Headwinds and *tailwinds* are additional examples of hackneyed jargon ...

*The United Kingdom's economic slowdown has been a **headwind** for major British corporations, though a weakening pound sterling could prove a **tailwind** for exports. In all, we believe British companies will provide attractive shareholder value in the year to come.*

... that could use fresher substitutes:

> *The United Kingdom's economic slowdown has **sapped the business momentum** of major British corporations. However, a weakening pound sterling could cheapen their exports and **thrust them into the global marketplace at a more competitive price**. In all, we believe British companies will provide attractive shareholder value in the year to come.*

Be Discerning about Nuance

Just as every penny of investor money counts and needs to be accounted for, so does every word with which you choose to communicate. This means being sensitive to word selections and the associations they conjure, and recognizing differences between closely related or nearly synonymous words and expressions. In the investment business, nuance is not an empty exercise in hairsplitting, but a delicate area of subtleties in which writers tread with the realization that even the finest distinctions they make can affect investors' interpretations and sentiments in a big way.

In short, nuance matters for two purposes: fine-tuning your vocabulary for accuracy, and connoting the proper associations.

Fine-tuning Your Vocabulary for Accuracy Accuracy is paramount for investment writing—even though, paradoxically, investing isn't wholly an enterprise of precision. It's a realm of approximations, estimates, and forecasts, and of projections (sometimes inaccurate), qualitative assessments, and "standard deviations." It is also a prisoner of fluid circumstances, of the unknown and unforeseen. Only a crystal ball would afford investors the precision that goes along with absolute certainty—and there are plenty of portfolio managers who would love to hear from you if you could find one.

All the same, investing is the kingdom of money, metrics, and accounting; of numerical expectations and well-defined strategies; and of manager stewardship and fiduciary responsibility. Investment writing therefore cannot be fuzzy or equivocal. It requires accuracy when reporting facts and clarity when providing interpretations of them. And it needs to be incisive: sharp in articulating ideas, surgical in logic, and penetrating in analysis. Verbal nuance—the art of finding *le mot juste* that captures exactly what you wish to say—is the bridge to achieving such standards.

Here are some common examples of subtle but noteworthy variations in word meanings to keep in mind:

- *Level off* or *plateau* versus *stabilize*

To "level off" or "plateau" is to cease to increase or decrease, whereas to "stabilize" is to become less volatile, converge on a point, or be unlikely to change for the time being. "Stabilize" carries a stronger, more definitive and reassuring association:

> *Energy prices are **leveling off** after their long ascent, yet some predict that they'll begin to decline soon. Meanwhile, the commodities market has **stabilized** following a bout of dramatic swings and seems to have entered lower-risk territory for now.*

- *Uptick, rise/increase,* and *spike*

  An "uptick" is a modest increase, a "rise" or "increase" is more substantial, and a "spike" is a sudden, steep rise.

  > *Any **uptick** in this gloomy market would be met with relief; a **rise**, with excitement; and a **spike**—with disbelief.*

- *Declines, dips, drops, drawdowns, downdrafts, pullbacks,* and *corrections*

  A "decline" is a general downward movement in the value of an investment. A "dip" is a decline often characterized as a buying opportunity with the assumption that there would be an eventual upswing. A "drop" can be used to signify a sharp, precipitous decline. A "drawdown" is a decline from peak to trough value as measured during a specific period. A "downdraft" is a strong downward turn following a break point. A "pullback" is the falling back of a value from its peak. And a "correction" implies a negative but temporary reversal in value—usually of at least 10 percent—that may be interrupting a broader upward trend in that value.

  > *What began as a **pullback** was then thought to be a **correction**, but now the picture is clear: The stock market suffered its greatest seven-month **drawdown** since the Great Depression. At the time, no one expected the seemingly unending bull market to meet such a **downdraft** so abruptly, but in hindsight, an inflection point was inevitable. Making things even more exasperating, the overall **decline** during this period was uneven, as some days were greeted with mild decreases whereas others saw violent **drops**. Throughout this period, investors who thought they were "buying the **dips**" lost a lot of money.*

■ *Fundamental, structural,* and *secular*

It's not uncommon to witness these three terms thrown around interchangeably, yet they are distinct.

Anything "fundamental" relates to the economics of a business (e.g., income statements, balance sheets, cash flows, and management quality), or of an industry or market (e.g., growth trends, supply and demand). It also pertains to elements affecting an economy at large (i.e., macroeconomic)—including employment, growth, a central bank's monetary policy, a government's fiscal policy, supply and demand, and inflation.

Anything "structural" concerns the way foundational elements of a business, industry, market, or economy relate to, or affect, each other in a constellation. For example, transformational changes in global commerce—the kind resulting from game-changing technology, dissipating trade barriers or tariff elimination—could be viewed as structural. Unemployment could also be considered structural if it's the result of a mismatch between the skills workers have and the skills the economy needs, rather than the product of a temporary downturn in the economic cycle (which would make it cyclical).

"Secular" is used to describe a trend or phenomenon persisting over a significant period—perhaps indefinitely—without being reversed or affected by shorter-term trends.

Hence:

> The pharmaceutical industry is poised to benefit from strong **fundamentals**: Higher life expectancy is spawning a growing population of seniors—a **secular** trend that will likely boost demand for healthcare and associated drugs, and increase industry revenues. However, an oncoming wave of drug patents are soon to expire and mount a **structural** challenge for companies whose business models are predicated on gleaning high profits from proprietary formulas. Our investment strategy focuses on manufacturers of cheaper generic drugs, which may be in a good position to capitalize on the expiration of those patents.

■ *Bullish* versus *constructive*

"Bullish" describes an investment view of unreserved optimism. "Constructive" is a tamer and more restrained version of bullish—still optimistic, but perhaps cautiously so, or sanguine (i.e., a positive outlook in an apparently difficult or questionable situation). It can also be used to describe a posture of building out an investment position in something.

> We're **bullish** on emerging markets, which have staged a vigorous recovery since last year's slump. Meanwhile, we remain **constructive** on select bank stocks in Europe that are beginning to exhibit resilient fundamentals in the face of a struggling financial sector throughout the region.

Connoting the Proper Associations Did we already mention that investing is sensitive business?

Investors, whose financial stakes hinge on your firm's better judgment, are highly attuned not just to what you write, but also to overtones and subtexts. Think of investment writing as a stream of lyrics whose words also shape the melody, unlike in actual music. (Fans of the soul genre may recall Arrested Development, the hip hop group that formed in the late 1980s, which was known for taking lyrics about harsh realities and cloaking them in deceptively buoyant tunes.)

As a junior writer, I was once tasked with drafting a question-and-answer segment featuring a fixed-income portfolio manager. The segment's purpose was to address investors' concerns about their bond holdings in an environment of rising interest rates. One of the questions elicited the manager's prediction: "How many times do you think the European Central Bank will hike rates in the months to come?" His thought was that the ECB would hike at least once.

Naturally, as in such matters, no forecast is surefire; one could only guess on the basis of cues. "We speculate that the ECB will hike at least once," I wrote in the draft I submitted to him for review. I got back an edited version with a furious comment scribbled on the first page: "We *never* speculate!" The verbal anathema was crossed out—and changed to *believe*.

Enter my first instructive encounter with nuance.

A case of fussiness, you may say? Not at all. Yes, to speculate is, in the sense I had intended, to theorize or conjecture. But as an investment activity, to speculate means to swing for the fences and take on high risk. And as someone for whom responsible risk-taking is a sacred principle, this portfolio manager did not want to associate himself with anything speculative—not even in the way of describing how he predicts—and invoke the wrong connotation with his clients. Fair enough.

Another example is the associative choice between *affect* and *impact*. The latter serves as an amplification of the former. And though *impact* is frequently summoned to the page in investment literature, it ought to be reserved for more severe repercussions or acute consequences of something, as in the following:

> *The rising costs of employee-benefit programs have progressively pinched profits and **affected** the balance sheets of some major corporations.*
>
> *Companies throughout the country are slashing benefits abruptly in a move that will likely **impact** millions in the workforce and require them to begin saving and investing much earlier for their golden years.*

On a related note of associations, some traits or actions that are less than admirable when applied to describe personal conduct can actually be virtuous in an investment context. To label someone an opportunist, for example, is to say that one seeks an advantage or something valuable without thinking about what's fair or right. But to characterize an investment strategy as opportunistic is perfectly acceptable; it is to distinguish that strategy as a carefully timed orchestration—one aimed at seizing a potentially short-lived benefit. Opportunistic strategies typically attempt to capitalize on the attractive price of an asset, or derive some larger gain from propitious (and possibly fleeting) market circumstances.

The idea of exploitation in human affairs carries similarly negative connotations of meanness or unfairness—and rightly so. But there's nothing undignified about describing an investment strategy as one that "exploits" anomalies in the market to gain an edge. In fact, there's a type of strategy in the hedge-fund world, known as "market neutral," designed to "exploit" differences in security prices—perhaps by assuming long and short positions in different securities of a certain category or sector—as a means of creating a hedge against market factors.

Investment writing may not always be poetic or literary, but it can certainly elevate one's appreciation for language and hone one's judgment for word choices.

Use Plain Language—Even If It's Technical

Technical nomenclature is no license for unintelligible, obscure, or exceedingly dense writing—nor does it legitimize the use of fanciful words or pretentious phrasing when simpler would do. Whether the level of your content is basic or advanced, keep your language plain and straightforward. Make sentences only as long as required by essence (that's to say, as short as possible), and don't construct them with too many clauses or complex syntax.

The U.S. Securities and Exchange Commission (SEC) provides a free handbook on how to create simple disclosure documents for investors, available at www.sec.gov/pdf/handbook.pdf. Though this handbook is geared toward U.S. securities laws, its principles of clarity are universally applicable to all manner of investment writing.

The SEC's handbook cites one example of a passage from a shareholder proxy statement for which it suggests a rewrite:

Before:
This Summary does not purport to be complete and is qualified in its entirety by the more detailed information contained in the Proxy Statement and the Appendices hereto, all of which should be carefully reviewed.
After:
Because this is a summary, it does not contain all the information that may be important to you. You should read the entire proxy statement and its appendices carefully before you decide how to vote.

Here's a separate example not cited in the SEC handbook but borrowed from a firm's retirement brochure:

Before:
Switching jobs qualifies you to be eligible for a rollover distribution, which is any distribution to an employee of all or any portion of the retirement-account balance to his or her credit in any number of plans, including, but not limited to, a 401(k), 403(b), and 457(b) plan.
After:
If you leave your current employer, you may transfer all the assets in your retirement account into a Rollover IRA. These assets include all amounts that you and your employer have contributed to your 401(k), 403(b), or 457(b) plan.

PIQUING INVESTORS' INTEREST

"I may not know a lot, but I think I know how to tell a story," Don Hewitt, television news producer, was fond of saying.[1] And he recognized the power of storytelling when founding the platinum-credentialed newsmagazine *60 Minutes*. Peter Jennings, former anchorman and managing editor of *ABC World News Tonight*, took the idea further and was said to bristle at any suggestion that viewers might not care about a well-told story. "*Make them care*," he'd urge his reporters.[2]

The merits of target-date funds? The non-correlative properties of insurance-linked securities? The case for municipal bonds? Some investment topics may not sound like the stuff of thrillers. Nonetheless, investors need to know. *Make them care.*

How do we do this? Consider one or any combination of the following:

- Forge a compelling storyline for your piece.
- Craft alluring headlines.
- Incorporate actual storytelling and anecdotes.
- Animate your writing with quotations, metaphors, and other references.

Forge a Compelling Storyline for Your Piece

Center your storyline on angles that are most consequential for the investor:

- What problem are you addressing and how do you suggest solving it?
- What investment objective are you helping to achieve?
- Is there an intellectually rousing aspect to the topic—perhaps a counter-intuitive element, an unexpected turn, or a surprising twist?
- Is it newsworthy or part of a greater, more significant story?

Part 2 of Chapter 5 on intellectual capital will address these angles at length from a content perspective.

Craft Alluring Headlines

Your headlines should intrigue readers by being specific, revealing a tip, giving a sense of immediacy or urgency, and exhibiting direct relevance to investors in order to draw them in. Here are some examples of recommended headlines and their less recommended counterparts:

Recommended	Less Recommended
Frontier markets: A short-term tactical play *(specific)*	Investment opportunities in frontier markets *(general)*
2 ways to position your portfolio for higher interest rates *(a quantified tip)*	A new era of higher interest rates *(insufficiently strong hook and no direct relevance)*
Enhancing diversification with sovereign local debt *(reflective of the benefit)*	The case for sovereign local debt *(run-of-the-mill and lacking in particulars)*
How the U.S. presidential election result may affect your portfolio *(focused and relevant)*	What's next following the U.S. presidential election? *(general and open-ended)*
4 stock sectors that could benefit from the fiscal stimulus *(a tip)*	How the fiscal stimulus could affect the stock market *(general)*
Upside down: Turning your asset allocation on its head *(provocative and original)*	Fundamentally reconsidering your asset allocation *(dull and uninspiring)*
How to invest for the remainder of 2018 *(targeted)*	2018 midyear outlook *(general)*

Headlines with puns and clever word games also increase your chances of garnering attention and sparking interest. For inspiration, consider an article by *The Economist* that addressed the precarious state of the London Interbank Offered Rate (LIBOR): Its title was "LIBOR Pains."[3] Or imagine a feature about investing in drone technology with a headline such as "Raising the stakes."

On a related note, keep your headlines short—up to roughly five-dozen characters, including spaces—and include keywords from your body copy to make them rank high in search engines.

Incorporate Storytelling and Anecdotes

A short story or anecdote is a good way to arouse investors' sense of curiosity. Some years ago, one author began his investment commentary on China with a recollection of his first journey to Beijing as a cash-strapped student: His budget small, he could only afford to book a cheap but punishing itinerary comprising four connecting flights from the United States—a total of 30 hours in transit.

Two others—Ian Bremmer, president of the Eurasia Group, and Lisa Shalett, then chief investment officer at Merrill Lynch Global Wealth Management—co-authored a paper in 2011 titled "New World, New Rules" in which they discussed "risk, opportunity and the seismic changes in the balance of power driving today's markets." They opened with a gripping account of the earthquake that struck the eastern coast of the United States that year—and tied it metaphorically to the rocky period the financial markets were going through at the time:

> *It happened after a new round of global financial turmoil, with Europe lurching deeper into its debt crisis, the Dow soaring and plunging by more than 400 points on six different occasions, and the United States receiving an unprecedented blow to its sovereign credit rating: New York and Washington, D.C., the centers of American financial and political power, were literally shaken. Chandeliers swung in the Capitol. Traders evacuated the New York stock exchange. The 5.8-magnitude earthquake on America's East Coast [on August 23, 2011,] actually caused little in the way of physical damage. But it was strong enough to reinforce a metaphor in the minds of people across the world: nothing seems to be stable anymore, not even the bedrock.*

As mentioned earlier, the interstices you allot to storytelling and anecdotes should be brief, as they are no more than a sideshow to your main topic. Ultimately, investment writing is for business—not literary—purposes, and it needs to be focused.

Animate Your Writing with Quotations, Metaphors, and Other References

To enliven investors' reading experiences, you can pepper your prose with provocative quotations, relatable references (such as from pop culture), and metaphors.

One author began an investment newsletter feature on diversification with a famous quote by Sir John Templeton to drive home the point: "The only investors who shouldn't diversify are those who are right 100% of the time." Another, in the opening of his paper, made an ironic reference to Halloween as the day that had happened to set the stage for the "spooked" financial markets of later months.

Apropos, metaphors are also terrific instruments for making complex subjects comprehensible. Chapter 6 (under the section titled "Use a Frame of Reference, Analogy, or Metaphor") features one such example.

As a reminder—and at the risk of sounding repetitive—there are types of investment literature, such as RFP responses or official letters, that are strictly formal and may not allow for much creative leeway. But for literature that can accommodate narratives—from bylined articles to commentary—seize the opportunity to be original and refreshing, and you'll stand a better chance of increasing readership.

THE VALUE OF A STYLE GUIDE FOR INVESTMENT WRITING

As a reference manual that sets standards for writing and content formatting, a style guide can offer multiple advantages for developing investment literature and communications. It contains answers to all the workaday questions writers routinely grapple with. It facilitates the composition process and saves deliberation time. And, as the go-to source of consultation for a company's stylistic principles and for everyone in the organization to abide by, it eliminates the need to provide repetitive training for writers, editors, and reviewers of investment material.

Yet the most valuable purpose of a style guide is to ensure the consistent application of the principles it prescribes. Why is such consistency important for investment writing? First, because inconsistency betrays carelessness, if not sloppiness—two characteristics any investment firm wouldn't want to be associated with. The responsibility and seriousness of managing money warrant a fastidious approach to detail, down to the most trivial (and yes, that includes the syntactic rules by which you capitalize letters and punctuate sentences).

Second, consistency breeds familiarity—and familiarity breeds comfort and contentment with the reading experience. Investors who consume your literature regularly come to expect the particular ways in which you formulate, lay out, and deliver content on the page. The more consistent you are, the more easily they'll be able to navigate and absorb what you write.

Lastly, consistency can make your content more recognizable by preserving distinct stylistic traits—verbal and visual. It can help differentiate your literature and imbue it with your company's identity.

KEY AREAS TO COVER IN YOUR FIRM'S STYLE RULES

Organizational style guides range from limited to comprehensive. Some are wholly proprietary—but developing them is a significant undertaking that's not always worth the effort. Others are part-proprietary while borrowing some principles from already-established guides such as *The Chicago Manual of Style, The Associate Press Stylebook, The New York Times Manual of Style and Usage,* or E. B. White and William Strunk Jr.'s *The Elements of Style.* And some companies simply choose to refer their writers to established guides as their primary sources of reference.

Regardless of which option you choose, be sure to cover a number of key areas when formulating in-house style rules. The following is by no means an exhaustive list—nor is it, in the case of syntax, wording and formatting, a recommendation to favor certain rules over others—but rather a general checklist to keep in mind.

Syntax, Wording, and Formatting

What rules do you follow within the margins of discretion for syntax? For example:

- *Capitalization*: Do you capitalize the first letter of every word in an organizational title (e.g., Vice President), functional title (Head of Capital Markets), subject title and/or subhead (The Case for Middle Market Loans)?
- *Punctuation*: Do you have punctuation preferences such as, for example, the Oxford comma, or a certain way of punctuating bulleted and numbered lists? Do you hyphenate any compound adjective, no matter how unambiguous (e.g., mid-cap stocks)? Do you prefer dashes to indicate number ranges (5%–10%) or the *to* preposition (5% to 10%)?
- *Terms and abbreviations*: In your guide, consider incorporating a comprehensive list of terms and abbreviations while indicating, where applicable, how and when they should be used. For example, what variations of specific terms do you prefer (e.g., selloff vs. sell-off)? What are your abbreviation conventions? For example, do you abbreviate U.S. state names by two-letter postal standards (e.g., FL for Florida) or the Associated Press format (Fla.)? Do you spell out well-known acronyms before abbreviating them (e.g., GDP, the U.K., NATO)?
- *Footnotes, endnotes, and glossary entries*: Which do you use, and when?
- *Numbers*: When do you spell them out, and when do you use digits? For example, some use digits only for 10 or higher. Some favor digits for all numbers above and below 10 in a single sentence, for consistency's sake.

And some favor digits when specifying capabilities (e.g., Our investment team has 3 economists and 4 analysts...).

- *Contractions*: Do you use them across the board, never at all, or only for specific words (e.g., *won't*, *it's*)?
- *Sources*: What format do you embrace for bibliographic citations and other sources? Here are two examples:

> *Doe, John.* The benefits of investing. *Publishing Company, Inc., 2017.*
> *Source: Imaginary Research Provider, Inc., as of [DATE]*

First-Person Pronouns and Possessives

What's your rule for an individual bylined author who uses the first-person pronoun or possessive in an article, research paper, commentary edition, or investor letter? Do you prefer the singular form (e.g., "I predict," "my view," "I believe") or plural one ("we predict," "our view")?

The singular form may work better when:

- The writing aims for a more personal tone.
- The individual is writing only behalf of herself rather than a group of people at the firm.
- It is disclosed that the views, predictions, and actions described in the piece represent the author's alone and are not necessarily those of the entire firm.
- You prefer to credit the author exclusively for what is written, even if the writing at hand is, or refers to, the product of collaboration.
- The author is more consequential individually than the group she or he represents.
- The author is a recognized, influential figure—perhaps in such a leadership role as the CEO, chief economist, chief investment officer, or head of a fund—whose name and reputation are enmeshed with the firm's identity.

Once you establish a set of rules for when to use the singular and plural forms, stick to them. If you find yourself moving from singular to plural within in the same piece of writing, contextualize the transition so that it's clear on whose behalf you're expressing the idea. (For an example, refer to the section titled "Investor Retention: It's All in the Communication" in Chapter 2.)

Chart Labeling

Charts are a terrific way of visualizing information, but they aren't always easy to grasp—especially in groups—because they can differ greatly. Some take the form of pies and others of lines or bars. They also differ in the data structures they depict, as well as in the relationships they exhibit between data series.

Every chart presents a new visual encounter that imposes additional strain on the reader. But you can make your investors' lives easier by standardizing a format of storytelling and labeling for all charts. Use your in-house style guide to establish such a uniform convention, so that at least you'll have an element of consistency across disparate charts that would render them more accessible.

Here are eight basic elements you can standardize:

1. The way you refer to charts within the body copy (e.g., "Chart 1," "Exhibit 1," "Display 1," etc.)
2. A story-driven title for each chart that contains a verb and explains the depicted narrative (e.g., "Home sales have risen in region A but remained stagnant in region B")
3. A description of what's mapped in the chart (e.g., "Seasonally adjusted rate of new home sales")
4. A vertical (Y) axis label (e.g., "Annual sales") and unit of account, if applicable (e.g., "in US$ millions")
5. A horizontal (X) axis label (e.g., "Date") and unit of account, if applicable ("Month/year")
6. A legend of data series on the bottom
7. Chart-related footnotes under the legend, if applicable
8. The source and "as-of" date of your information (which, given the secondary nature of their importance, can be relegated to the very bottom, under the legend and footnotes)

Figure 4.1 shows one example.

International Considerations

Does your firm cater to a multinational clientele? Formulate writing guidelines to make your content suitable for offshore audiences and/or translations to other languages. Alternatively, create a separate version for such audiences.

Here are some factors to consider:

- *Idioms*: You may need to refrain from using local idioms that are not translatable or that may not be properly interpreted in other cultures (e.g., "mom-and-pop shops" or "experience/achievements under one's belt")

FIGURE 4.1 How to format a chart using consistent elements

Exhibit 1: Home sales have risen in Region A but remained stagnant in Region B

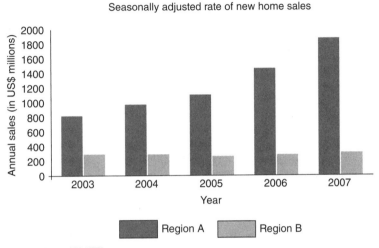

Source: X, as of [DATE]

- *Spelling and wording*: Consider regional differences in spelling and wording, such as the differences between American and British English spelling (e.g., *center* vs. *centre*, respectively) and wording (e.g., *among* vs. *amongst*). You may even want to establish an official reference dictionary for each region.
- *Dates*: Follow the appropriate date format of a region, such as the American numerical format of MONTH/DAY/YEAR or the European numerical format of DAY/MONTH/YEAR.
- *Currencies*: Currencies that have international counterparts with identical names may require national specification. Thus, you could specify $100 as, say, US$100 to distinguish it from Canadian dollars (C$100), New Zealand dollars (NZ$100) or Australian dollars (AU$100).
- *Ethnocentric references*: Consider avoiding such words as *foreign* or *alien* (as in "foreign investments" or "resident aliens") and using more cosmopolitan substitutes (e.g., "non-U.S. investments," "residents with international citizenships"). The exception to this rule is foreign exchange, also known as FX in acronym form, which is a common way to address the international currency market.

Inessential Words

To tighten your copy, include guidelines about eliminating words that are redundant or outright unnecessary. *Time period* is a common example, whereas just *time* or *period* would do, as in "Markets have risen during that time," or "Markets have risen over that period."

Level is another word often used superfluously, as when referring to "inflation levels," "debt levels," "unemployment levels," or "valuation levels." Incidentally, *rate* is a more proper numerical descriptor of, say, an inflation *rate* of X%. But *level* is nowhere needed when writing that "inflation has remained above average," that "a company raised its debt," that "unemployment has declined," or that "valuations are attractive."

Finally, incorporate general guidelines for replacing such wordy phrases as "at this point in time" with a simple "currently," "presently," or "now."

Cumbersome Constructions

Include a cautionary note about avoiding complicated sentences. One example is the common proclivity to stack up too many noun modifiers.

For example:

Before: Developed- and emerging-market sovereign and corporate bond spreads are widening.

After: The spreads of sovereign and corporate bonds are widening in both developed and emerging markets.

Another example is the construction of long-winded sentences with more than two clauses or complex syntax:

Before: Since the public market for real estate investing in Southeast Asia is still in its growing stage—instruments such as commercial mortgage-backed securities (CMBS) are not nearly as prevalent as in the United States—relative yields are attractively high, though we expect them to decline over time as the public market develops.

After: The public market for real estate investing in Southeast Asia is still in its growing stage: Instruments such as commercial mortgage-backed securities (CMBS) are not nearly as prevalent as in the United States. For this reason, relative yields are attractively high, though we expect them to decline over time as the public market develops.

Legal Considerations

Your in-house style guide is a good place to explain and demonstrate the legal restrictions on the way writers can articulate the firm's perspectives, couch product offerings, and dispense advice. Chapter 7 addresses this subject in detail.

Tone

This one is tricky, since tone is a hazy realm. Still, you can provide some direction to help writers fine-tune their voice by including the following elements in your corporate guide:

1. *A word palette*: Word palettes are essentially lists of commonly used words. They are small but stylistically representative samples of the vocabulary you'll often enlist for your writing, and can serve as a proxy for the voice of your firm. A word palette is useful as a prescriptive guideline featuring concrete examples, and you can pair it with an "anti-palette" (i.e., a corresponding list of synonymous words that *should not* be used) to distinguish your desired tone.

   As an example, here's a small portion of a word palette that could suit a firm wishing to maintain a warm, common touch with retail investors:

Prefer the Following:	Avoid the Following:
Get	Obtain
Advice	Recommendation
To use/apply	To leverage
Find the best way to … Make the most of … Make more efficient …	Optimize
Clients	Customers

2. *Company attributes*: List the characteristics of your firm to give writers a reference of values and ideals with which to approach their writing and aim for the appropriate style.

   Here's one example:

What We Are:	What We Aren't:
Opinionated	Neutral/hesitant/always hedging our bets
Innovative and original	Conventional
Focused	Rambling
Enticing	Dull
Flexible and responsive	Cookie-cutter
Attuned to client needs	Centered only on what we offer

Along similar lines, your guide can describe the types of balance to achieve in your firm's communications to investors. For example:

- Be confident but not arrogant.

    Confident: We invest in Asia with high conviction, given recent economic indicators in the region.

    Arrogant: It's obvious to us why we should invest in Asia: Just look at the region's economic indicators.

- Be conversational without appearing dumbed-down, chatty, slangy, or overly casual.

    Conversational: Sure, we think the risk of greater inflation is fairly high—but the current inflation rate is acceptable.

    Slangy: Yeah, we think the risk of inflation is pretty high—but the inflation rate now is okay.

You may grant more leeway for the casual style when publicizing transcriptions of spoken conversations—such as the kind that appear in written question-and-answer (Q&A) documents—to preserve the original voice of the speaker.

- Be authoritative without sounding patronizing, presumptuous, or lawyerly.

    Authoritative: The acceleration of capital flows into aerospace and defense stocks leads us to one conclusion: Investors believe that military expenditures will rise.

    Patronizing: Investors appear to believe that military expenditures will rise. What other conclusion would you reach by observing the acceleration of capital flows into aerospace and defense stocks?

    Lawyerly: It is the acceleration of capital flows into aerospace and defense stocks that leads us to posit with relative confidence, notwithstanding potentially contradictory assertions, that investors believe that military expenditures will rise.

- Show that we're a large and resourceful firm that has earned experience with many clients, but stress that we are committed to each individual.
- Imply that though we've grown to manage billions in assets, we know the value of every single unit of currency.

3. *Clients' characteristics*: If you have a good read on the nature of your firm's clients—whether anecdotally or through proper research—describe it. Writers who use your guide will have a clearer sense of whom they're writing for and adjust their tone accordingly.

For example, you may describe your clients as:

- **Curious and informed,** meaning that they thirst for information, consider it carefully when making decisions, keep abreast of current events, and want their intellect respected;
- **Busy,** meaning that they lead demanding lives, only have time for what's essential, and value brevity; or
- **Working professionals,** meaning that they have labored to create the wealth they invest and wish to be taken seriously.

4. *External references*: Specify a financial publication—whether it's a scholarly economics journal or the investment or business section of a common newspaper—that can serve as a frame of reference for writers to achieve your firm's desired tone and level of technical vocabulary.

Principles for Creating Scannable Copy

Counsel writers on making information digestible at a glance—or the gist of a story readily apparent—especially when it comes to long-form literature (such as research papers, brochures, or commentary) by:

- Prefacing with a bulleted executive summary in the beginning, perhaps with a predetermined word-count limit for each bullet
- Breaking up large blocks of text with subheads
- Using shaded sidebars containing additional or explanatory material
- Placing callouts (also known as pull quotes) of key thoughts from the main text, in large fonts, throughout the piece—whether on or within the margins
- Using charts and illustrations to depict information-rich ideas

Addressing Common Language Mistakes

Lastly, advise writers on the common mistakes they should avoid in grammar, word choices, and syntax. Without getting into detailed linguistic explanations, here are examples of words and phrases that are indistinguishably perceived and often confused with one another:

- *Less than* vs. *fewer than*
  (We're taking **less** risk by holding **fewer** stocks in our portfolio.)
- *More than* vs. *over*
  (We've invested **over** a period of **more than** six months.)
- *Based on . . .* vs. *on the basis of . . .*

(**On the basis** of our analyst's recommendation, we're pursuing a certain investment strategy. This strategy is **based on** four tenets.)

■ *Past* vs. *last*

(Over the **past** few months, we've changed our outlook. As a result, we decided to exit a key position we had taken **last** week.)

A PARTING NOTE ON STYLE

The inevitable conclusion when it comes to investment writing is that style and substance are entwined. From vocabulary to formatting, from overall tone to the way complex subjects are approached and elucidated, style has two legs: one planted in content and the other in presentation.

In other words, style bestrides a dividing line between *manner* and *matter*. It's a manner of expression and personification, but it is also a content element and a strategic communication tool. Writers can weigh its use according to what best serves an intent or purpose in a specific situation with a particular type of investor. Ideally, investment writing should reflect individual and organizational identities while employing suitable conventions of language and presentation to produce a message that is accurate and intelligible and that drives the intended result.

NOTES

1. Don Hewitt, "Tell Me a Story: Fifty Years and 60 Minutes in Television," October 1, 2002.
2. "Peter Jennings, Reporter," ABC News, August 10, 2005. Retrieved on June 6, 2017, at youtube.com/watch?v=KGGael2–8EE&feature=youtu.be. At the time marker of 1:24:20, Tom Nagorski (Senior Producer, *ABC World News Tonight*) says: "Peter disliked intensely any suggestion that the audience isn't going to care about, or be interested in, a story. He felt it's an example of laziness if you said 'I can't imagine the audience can care about that.' He said: 'Make them care.'"
3. "LIBOR Pains: A Crucial Interest-Rate Benchmark Faces a Murky Future," *The Economist*, August 3, 2017.

CHAPTER 5

Developing an Architecture of Investment Content

Having covered the journalistic principles, strategic purposes, and stylistic considerations of investment writing in previous chapters, you are halfway ready to express your ideas through quality content. Halfway, because before you scratch that itch and finally begin to write, you will need to:

1. Establish an architecture of investment content for your firm.
2. Review the purposes served by different forms of content, as well as effective editorial approaches to each.
3. Understand the legal considerations to keep in mind as you write.

Symbolically, you are also about halfway through this book. The second half you've just begun will cover all these issues and carry you straight to the blank page that, presumably, you cannot wait to fill.

Let's start with establishing an architecture of investment content.

What is this architecture, exactly? It's a method of classifying, organizing, and packaging all manner of written material (also known as collateral) intended for investor consumption. With a content architecture in place, you'll have a system of rationalizing your collection of writings and assembling them into an array of literature and communications—those to be widely published and those to be delivered to select audiences.

It's worth qualifying this discussion with two caveats as preface.

First, no single architectural framework of content fits all. Larger firms typically churn out voluminous content and may espouse more elaborate architecture featuring a breadth of publications—each with its own purpose. A more limited variety of publications may suffice for smaller firms that produce less content, or at least fewer types of it.

Second, semantics and conventions vary for composing, categorizing, and labeling different forms of content. For instance, what constitutes a "whitepaper" or "brochure" for one firm may not for another. Firms differ in their editorial philosophy—as well they should, since no two firms are alike—and follow varied approaches to content development.

Nonetheless, I'll attempt to propose a framework of content organization and formulation that can either be mimicked or serve as a standard from which to derive adaptations that would suit specific firms.

Investment content typically falls into the following five buckets we'll cover throughout this chapter:

1. Foundational literature
2. Intellectual capital
3. Educational literature
4. Digital and social media
5. Shareholder communications

PART 1: FOUNDATIONAL LITERATURE

The most essential type of literature for any investment firm is the kind that describes investment products and capabilities. Known in some quarters as foundational literature, it is the must-have written companion for all sales and marketing efforts without which, quite simply, you cannot win new investors or obtain the endorsements of advisors and consultants.

Four of the most crucial forms of foundational literature are firm-overview and investment-capabilities brochures, strategy and product profiles, responses to requests for proposals (RFPs), and pitch books. You may also develop case studies and topical brochures as optional content.

Let's review some conceptual and writing guidelines for each of these six types of foundational literature.

Firm-Overview and Investment-Capabilities Brochures

As an introduction to who you are and a bird's-eye view of what you offer, firm-overview and investment-capabilities brochures are your starting point. For large firms, whose business runs broad and deep, it makes sense to separate the "firm overview" part from the "capabilities" part and create two or more independent brochures. (Some firms have a capabilities brochure for each line of business, such as equities, fixed income, alternative investments, and multi-asset-class strategies.)

For smaller firms, one consolidated brochure containing a firm overview and a description of investment capabilities could work better, especially when there isn't enough fodder on either to constitute a standalone piece.

If your firm caters to both private and institutional clients, you may wish to create separate versions for each, considering the major differences in the needs of those audiences and the products they can access. (The writing examples you'll encounter next will assume one version for both audiences—but only for illustrative purposes.)

The Firm Overview The firm overview could include any pertinent information relating to the enterprise as a whole, such as:

- A general description of the company and its offerings, mission statement, founding principle, and overarching philosophy
- A high-level overview of the company's areas of expertise, technical capabilities, product lines, and organizational structure
- The company's workforce size, office locations, and geographic reach of business
- A brief summary of the company's client profile, including the types of private and/or institutional clients served, their geographic locations, and an aggregation of clients by the tenure of their relationship with the company (see the example that follows)
- The company's total assets under management, as well as a breakdown by asset class (e.g., equities, fixed income, alternative strategies), client type (e.g., individuals, endowments, foundations, corporate sponsors of employee-retirement plans), or product (e.g., hedge funds, municipal-bond funds, private equity funds)
- A brief summary of the company's history and key milestones (whether verbally; in pictorial form, such as a visual timeline; or both)
- An introduction to the company's leadership team, perhaps including short biographies of key executives

---

EXAMPLE OF SELECT PARTS OF A FIRM'S OVERVIEW

InvestorPro started out nearly 50 years ago as a small boutique operation managing individuals' lifetime savings and helping them retire with dignity. Today we are a global investment firm of more than 3,000 professionals serving thousands of individuals and institutions in 20 countries with one mission: to help clients achieve their financial objectives (Figure 5.1).

(Continued)

FIGURE 5.1 Within 4 decades, InvestorPro has grown to encompass 4 continents

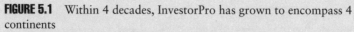

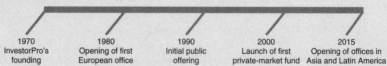

| 1970 | 1980 | 1990 | 2000 | 2015 |
| InvestorPro's founding | Opening of first European office | Initial public offering | Launch of first private-market fund | Opening of offices in Asia and Latin America |

At InvestorPro, we believe that skilled managers with access to proprietary research can add value to client portfolios. With more than US$470 billion in assets under management, we offer investment strategies spanning the risk/return spectrum across geographies, investment styles, and asset classes, including equities, fixed income, alternative assets, and private markets (Table 5.1).

TABLE 5.1 We offer a wide-ranging selection of strategies in support of investment objectives

Equity Strategies	Fixed-Income Strategies	Alternative Strategies	Private-Market Strategies
InvestorPro Domestic Equity Strategies	InvestorPro Global Bond Strategies	InvestorPro Long/Short Equity Strategies	InvestorPro Infrastructure Funds
InvestorPro Global Equity Strategies	InvestorPro Municipal Bond Strategies	InvestorPro Multi-Strategy Funds	InvestorPro Private Equity Funds
InvestorPro Index Funds	InvestorPro European Loan Strategies	InvestorPro Commodity Strategies	InvestorPro Private Real Estate Funds

We cater to a variety of individuals, high-net-worth investors, and institutions, which include corporate and government sponsors of defined-benefit retirement plans, insurance companies, endowments, foundations, and sovereign wealth funds. The longevity of our institutional relationships, in particular, is testament to the quality of our service—and to our clients' reliance on us to support and strengthen their financial well-being (Table 5.2).

TABLE 5.2 InvestorPro has earned numerous longstanding relationships with institutional clients

Number of InvestorPro Clients	Tenure
398 clients	Up to 5 years
207 clients	5–10 years
105 clients	10–15 years
78 clients	15–30 years
21 clients	30+ years

An Overview of Investment Capabilities The introduction of your firm's investment capabilities—whether in a standalone brochure or as part of a larger piece that includes the firm overview—is a deeper, more granular dive into a firm's specific line or lines of business. It can include detailed descriptions of any combination of the following:

- The products offered within those lines of business, as well as the overarching investment philosophy, approach, and organizational culture that bind them
- Assets under management within business lines and, optionally, a breakdown by asset class, product, or client type (as explained in the firm-overview section)
- The management teams' organization structure and technical expertise
- Operational resources (such as technology; trading, research, and analytical capabilities; and other features of organizational infrastructure)
- Distinguishing advantages or characteristics—such as heritage, experience, geographic reach, breadth of resources, or industry relationships—that make the firm remarkable (as explained later in this chapter)

Let's revert to the fictitious example of InvestorPro. If to judge by its assets under management, number of personnel, and disparate product lines, this imaginary firm occupies a place on the upper end of mid-size investment outfits—at least by Wall Street standards—that could benefit from separate capabilities brochures for each of its four lines of business: equities, fixed income, alternatives, and private markets. Here's how select portions of its equity capabilities brochure could be written:

A VARIETY OF STRATEGIES FOR THE EQUITY INVESTOR

InvestorPro has been investing in stocks on behalf of its clients for nearly five decades. Today our equity division alone manages more than $150 billion in assets across three groups of strategies:

1. **Fundamental strategies** that use economic, sector, and company research as the basis of stock selection
2. **Passive (index) strategies** that provide low-cost alternatives for gaining exposure to various market segments by closely tracking representative baskets of securities
3. **Quantitative strategies** that use proprietary algorithms backed by active management and research to drive the investment process

With the realization that investors could benefit from diversified, professionally managed portfolios to achieve their objectives, we have designed our strategies to run the gamut of market capitalizations and geographic destinations (Table 5.3).

A Disciplined Approach to Investing Backed by Robust Research

Drawing on a wealth of proprietary research, InvestorPro's experienced portfolio managers invest with a long-term perspective while taking advantage of near-term opportunities. They follow rigorous processes that bring their experience to bear on each investment decision. These processes are designed to keep expenses down—and keep their strategies true to style—in an effort to meet the needs of investors with varied goals, risk tolerances, and time horizons.

A Blend of Independence and Collaboration

Our portfolio-management teams operate independently in an organizational structure that grants them the autonomy of expressing diverse views and pursuing varied strategies. Yet our teams are also joined at the hip through a collaborative culture—one that enables them to pollinate each other with knowledge and ideas. This culture enables them to augment their points of view with interdisciplinary perspectives, discern protean themes affecting equity performance, and potentially capitalize on market trends.

State-of-the-Art Trading Capabilities

InvestorPro's equity division is powered by 20 traders at desks located in North and Latin America, Europe, and Asia. They operate a cutting-edge trading platform featuring technologies and analytical capabilities that the firm has developed in-house and refined over decades.

These technologies promote swift and efficient trading, maximize access to stock liquidity from all locations, help us optimize transactions, and reduce the costs of trade execution for our clients.

TABLE 5.3 InvestorPro's Equity Strategies at a Glance, by Geography

Developed-Market Equity Strategies	Global Equity Strategies	Emerging-Market Equity Strategies
Strategy A (fundamental)	Strategy D (fundamental)	Strategy G (fundamental)
Strategy B (quantitative)	Strategy E (index)	Strategy H (fundamental)
Strategy C (index)	Strategy F (index)	Strategy I (index)

InvestorPro's Advantages in Equity Investing

Our equity division enjoys a number of distinguishing features, including:

- **Access to key decision-makers:** InvestorPro's relationships with management teams of companies in which we invest—as well as with leaders of industry and government officials—help us conduct exhaustive research and gain penetrating insights into country, company, and business fundamentals.
- **Global resources:** Our international footprint in research and trading enables us to react to market developments and opportunities quickly. It also allows us to synthesize the benefits of scale with

(Continued)

a regional focus through our local presence in various locations throughout the world.

- **Diverse equity platform:** Our blend of active and passive offerings—and our diverse, experienced pool of talent—provide clients with a multifaceted platform of investment philosophies, ideas, and strategies to consider toward achieving their objectives.

Packaging Options As earlier mentioned—and to be reinforced as a motif throughout this chapter—there is no single right way to divide, package, and bundle investment content, including foundational literature. You may create a single brochure outlining your firm's overview and investment capabilities in one. You may create one brochure for each. Or you can produce one overview brochure and a series of capabilities brochures—one for each line of business. If a particular line of business is sizable—such as, for example, "alternative investments"—you may consider a separate brochure for each sub-line (e.g., currencies, commodities, hedge funds, etc.).

Another option is to create a one-page summary overview of your firm containing only the most essential introductory information, and another one-page overview of investment offerings at a glance (of the kind shown in the InvestmentPro example of capabilities). Those two modules can then be used as introductory standalone pieces or combined with strategy profiles (explained next) to create an overview-and-capabilities package à la carte. If your firm's investment offerings are too numerous to fit on a one- or two-page format, consider producing an accordion-fold brochure that can accommodate multiple such pages. As an aside, at-a-glance pieces are useful as handouts (i.e., "leave-behind" marketing materials) with clients and intermediaries because of their capacity to condense a lot of information in an absorbable fashion—especially for those who only want to give them a hurried look.

In short, the empty canvas is yours for the filling. Cover your firm and its offerings fully while satisfying the needs of thorough and hasty readers alike.

Strategy and Product Profiles

Now that you've provided investors and their advisors with an overhead view of your organization and capabilities, it's time to describe the specific investment strategies and products on offer. The most effective way to do this is through summary profiles on each individual offering that distill the most important information an investor should know. (RFP responses, addressed next, provide more detailed information.)

A prefatory note on semantics before we begin: *Strategy, fund,* and *product* are often conflated and used interchangeably when applied to written literature, but they are technically different. A *strategy profile* describes an investment strategy proper—one that can be offered through any number of *investment vehicles* highlighted in the profile, as we'll review in the section on "Investment Terms and Parameters at a Glance." Together, a strategy and vehicle constitute a product for the investor to access. Hence, a *product profile* describes an investment strategy delivered through a specific type of vehicle, such as a fund.

When developing strategy and product profiles, remember the words of Shmuel Harlap—a name that may strike you as obscure, unless you are familiar with Israel's circle of venture capitalists. Dr. Harlap was among the first to invest in Mobileye, a company that developed breakthrough technology to improve the safety of motor vehicles and be used in the assembly of driverless cars. When Mobileye was acquired by Intel Corporation years later, he reaped US\$1.1 billion on his investment, and had the following to say:

> *I made a strategic decision when I invested that so long as [both of Mobileye's co-founders] are managing the company, I won't sell a single share. I believed in the technology and—no less, if not more so—in their talents, and in their word.*[1]

Bingo! Product, talent, and integrity: Into one brief statement, Harlap managed to capture the trifecta investors bet on when entrusting their managers with money. They are the three prongs of any investment proposition and should serve as the basis of its articulation. In that spirit, include most if not all of the following in your strategy and product profiles:

The Strategy's or Product's Definition   Your profile should open with an "elevator pitch" of your strategy or product: a pithy, succinct description of its nature and purpose. Surprisingly, many profiles fail to deliver that pitch effectively at the very beginning, where it most counts.

Here's a less-than-perfect example of a strategy's definition by a firm that shall remain nameless:

> *Our European Value strategy seeks to capture misvaluations through an investment process that integrates fundamental and quantitative research to determine expected returns in an effort to generate a performance premium.*

This muddled definition suffers from a few critical gaps. Foremost among them: There isn't even a single reference to stocks—a puzzling omission when you consider that it's an equity strategy in the first place. And this is just one of countless examples frequently encountered, a poster child for the flawed strategy definitions out there.

Cheer up, comrades, for a solution is at hand: Simply use one inclusive formula for all your definitions—and stick to it. You'd be surprised to see how effectively it can work.

Here is a suggested formula for strategy definitions:

[STRATEGY NAME] is [STRATEGY TYPE] that seeks to [STRAT-EGY OBJECTIVE] by following [STRATEGY BLUEPRINT] and emphasizing [STRATEGY FOCUS]

By molding the foregoing example into this formula, we get a more coherent definition of the strategy that covers all the elementary bases:

European Value is an international equity strategy that aims to generate excess returns (or alpha) by identifying discounted, publicly traded stocks throughout Europe. To accomplish its objective, the strategy's management team follows a process that integrates fundamental and quantitative research in order to determine a company's expected returns. The strategy focuses on companies with low price-to-sales (P/S) ratios.

Here's a hypothetical, more descriptive example of the formula in action:

InvestorPro Loan Plus is a fixed-income strategy that seeks a high level of current income and capital preservation by investing in a diversified portfolio of senior secured loans. To achieve its objective, the strategy centers on identifying corporate borrowers that exhibit strong credit fundamentals. It favors companies that generate cash flows consistently; have quality management teams, preferably with experience managing leveraged balance sheets; and have solid collateral coverage. The strategy focuses on senior loans domiciled in the United States, though it may also invest in select loans originated in Canada.

This formula can also be used with products (which, as mentioned before, are strategies delivered through specific vehicles that make them accessible to the investor), such as funds:

[FUND NAME] is [FUND TYPE] that seeks to [FUND OBJEC-TIVE] by following [FUND STRATEGY] and emphasizing [FUND FOCUS]

Consider this example of an imaginary real-estate investment strategy offered through an open-end commingled fund vehicle:

InvestorPro Global Premier is a private real estate fund that seeks to provide a stable rate of return—primarily from income, with modest price appreciation—over the long term. To achieve its objective, the fund's management team looks to acquire and hold prime properties, diversified by type and location, in major metropolitan areas around the world. The team focuses on Class A multifamily communities, office buildings, commercial malls, warehouses, and storage facilities.

You may need to use variations of the formula to suit particular funds, such as in the following two examples.

EXAMPLE #1: FUNDS OR STRATEGIES WITH SELF-EXPLANATORY NAMES

Oftentimes, the name of a fund or strategy will also reveal its type. In that case, begin with [FUND NAME], skip [FUND TYPE], move straight to [FUND OBJECTIVE], and continue from there. Thus:

The InvestorPro Private Equity Partners fund seeks attractive, risk-adjusted returns over the long haul from a portfolio of companies acquired through privately negotiated transactions. The fund targets buyout opportunities on the lower end of the middle market across a range of industries globally, with a focus on Latin America and Asia.

EXAMPLE #2: PASSIVE PRODUCTS

Many index and exchange-traded funds (ETFs) are designed to track an index or basket of securities rather than follow an independent,

(Continued)

idiosyncratic strategy. The absence of such a strategy renders [FUND STRATEGY] and [FUND FOCUS] irrelevant, as in the following:

> *The InvestorPro International Bond ETF is a fixed-income fund that seeks to track the investment performance of an index composed of bonds outside the United States denominated in local (non-U.S. dollar) currencies.*

For quasi-passive (also known as "smart beta") ETFs that combine index tracking with proprietary-weighting methodologies, you can use the [FUND STRATEGY] part of the formula to describe in broad terms what the methodology is:

> *The InvestorPro U.S. Dividend Tracker ETF is an equity fund that seeks to track the investment results of dividend-paying companies in the broad U.S. equity market. To achieve its objective, the fund invests in an index that is dividend-weighted to reflect the proportionate share of the aggregate cash dividends each component company is projected to pay in the coming year. This projection is based on the most recently declared dividend per share.*

The Investment Philosophy After defining your strategy or product, you will need to explain the investment philosophy behind it. The philosophy question is not one of abstract musings or thought experiments, but rather a concrete question of financial conviction:

> *How does your management team believe it can make money by investing in X?*

A pretty straightforward question, you may think. Yet many miss the mark when attempting to answer it. Here are two recommended guidelines for getting the investment philosophy right:

1. Begin by stating a belief or view (e.g., "The management team believes...," "In the team's view," etc.). The initial reference to a subjective viewpoint, right then and there, will help set you on the right course of articulating your philosophy.

2. Avoid falling into the common trap of making the case for the investment in question. An investment philosophy isn't about *why you believe X is an attractive investment*, but rather *how you believe you can identify investment opportunities in X and harvest returns*. There's a difference.

If investors inquire about the philosophy of, say, a private equity fund, they aren't interested in hearing you extoll the virtues of private equity as a potentially lucrative investment destination. (There are other opportunities for you to do so, explained separately in Part 2 on intellectual capital.) Instead, they would like to know how you think you could wring value from private equity and extract returns. Is it by avoiding market segments with intense buyout competition? Focusing on secondary-market opportunities to which you have privileged access? Concentrating on niche enterprises in which your firm has operational knowledge? Essentially, investors would want to understand your particular approach to investing in private equity and how it differs from the rest.

Here are some examples of satisfactory—and, as a point of reference, unsatisfactory—investment philosophies:

Investment Philosophies

	Satisfactory Investment Philosophy	Unsatisfactory Investment Philosophy
A private-equity investment strategy	The management team believes that it can garner returns from private equity transactions by pursuing deals that are attractively valued, entail moderate leverage, and present opportunities for operational change in acquired businesses operating in niche industries.	The management team finds that private equity is experiencing burgeoning growth amid lenient credit conditions and may therefore present an attractive opportunity for investors.

Investment Philosophies

	Satisfactory Investment Philosophy	Unsatisfactory Investment Philosophy
A large-cap equity investment strategy	In the team's view, large-cap stock prices don't always reflect business catalysts (such as a management change or reorganization) that have the potential to help a company achieve higher growth. By identifying such catalysts, the team aims to monetize potential increases in the valuations of companies.	Large-cap stocks can be a solid destination for investors because they represent established businesses that command significant market share and tend to be less volatile. For this reason, the management team believes they may serve as a foundation (i.e., core allocation) of an investor's stock portfolio.
A real-estate investment strategy	The team believes that by investing in quality real estate in major metropolitan areas, it can gain exposure to more liquid assets, profit from diverse tenant bases, and benefit from stronger resilience to market cycles.	The management team sees real estate as a strong investment because it has the potential to appreciate in value in areas of growing demand and limited supply.

Investment Philosophies

	Satisfactory Investment Philosophy	Unsatisfactory Investment Philosophy
A corporate-bond investment strategy	The team espouses a two-part approach to outperforming its benchmark and mitigating the risk of losses from bankruptcies: 1. Making investment decisions solely on the basis of credit fundamentals of debt issuers—irrespective of the broader credit environment; and 2. Diversifying investments among issuers of different sectors. The team views rigorous fundamental analysis and firsthand proprietary research as paramount for evaluating individual issuers.	The management team views bonds as an appealing opportunity to earn income and enjoy potential capital appreciation at the same time.
A commodities investment strategy	The management team believes that by focusing on certain commodity markets that are less efficient than others, it can exploit price inefficiencies through arbitrage to reap incremental returns.	In the management team's view, commodities can serve as an effective source of diversification, because their behavior tends to be uncorrelated to other assets.

The investment philosophy you articulate is also a very good differentiator, because it reveals not just *what* you think, but *how* you think—the intellectual rationale behind your strategy. For more on how an investment philosophy fits into an array of potentially differentiating characteristics, see the later section titled "Distinguishing Features or Advantages."

The Investment Process   By now, investors have a general idea of your strategy. They understand everything we've covered up to now:

- The type of strategy you're offering (i.e., what it invests in, and how)
- The strategy's objective (i.e., what it seeks to achieve)
- The strategy's blueprint (i.e., the general plan of action for achieving its objective)
- The strategy's focus (i.e., the specific area it emphasizes to achieve its objective)
- The management team's philosophy (i.e., how the team believes it can identify opportunities and make money by investing in X)

So far, so good.

But how does your management team actually go about putting the strategy to practice? Once the portfolio managers, research analysts, and traders assume positions at their desks—presumably after a requisite shot of morning caffeine—what is their *modus operandi*?

Welcome to the investment process—a set of activities undertaken by the team to conduct research, identify, and analyze opportunities, make "buy" and "sell" decisions, execute trades, manage risks, and direct all other aspects of a portfolio.

(1) Common Elements of the Investment Process   Investment processes vary greatly by the type of strategy pursued. But many strategies—especially those that aren't strictly algorithmic and entail some human intervention—share a basic anatomy of skeletal elements that warrant articulation. These elements may include any variation of the following:

1. *An investment universe:* The management team of a strategy may operate within a delineated perimeter of investment possibilities, known as a universe, that it circumscribes for itself. A universe is what helps the team maintain focus and begin the initial qualification of target candidates for investing on the basis of preliminary criteria.

   Typically, strategies that focus on a single class of assets have a defined universe. An equity strategy, for example, could define as its universe stocks that fall within a range of market capitalizations, or that answer to other criteria of region, industry, or index inclusion. A fixed-income strategy could limit itself to a universe of bonds of a specific type of issuer (such as a government or corporation), a particular region, or a certain grade of creditworthiness. One firm launched a global energy exploration fund that derived its universe from geological information on hundreds of oil and natural-gas basins around the world.

Some management teams (such as those of asset-allocation, multi-strategy, and hedge funds, or of other unconstrained strategies) plot investments across asset classes and may not wish to limit themselves to a universe. Instead, they may prefer to shape their investment decisions by other criteria—financial, economic, political, and so on—while maintaining the freedom to invest anywhere they please.

2. *Research, opportunity sourcing, and screening:* This element pertains to how a management team puts its philosophy to practice. What ideas come to mind in the quest for prospective investments? Where and how does the team look to uncover them? Does it aim to discern a pattern, market development, or anomaly? Does it favor overlooked opportunities that skulk beneath the radar of most investors in obscure areas of the market? What eligibility criteria—qualitative or numerical—do prospects need to satisfy for consideration?

   Some teams source opportunities in the public domain—the stock or bond markets, for instance—using widely available information. Some also draw on firsthand research, such as when meeting with the leaders of entities in which they invest. Others, including managers of private funds and international strategies, source opportunities privately from relationships with industry contacts and government connections, or from proprietary databases.

   In many cases, management teams face a swath of opportunities in the exploratory phases of an investment process, then progressively narrow their focus on targets of high interest that meet more specific qualifications.

3. *Due diligence and analysis:* When pinpointing opportunities that passed the preliminary screening, the management team will usually inspect them before making a decision to invest. They may evaluate the opportunity by region, country, sector, industry, asset, financial profile, or any combination of these factors. The analysis could be top-down (in the case of the first four) and/or bottom-up; manual and/or algorithmic; qualitative and/or quantitative.

4. *Investment determination:* To reach a final verdict on deploying capital for a specific investment, the team may follow a rules-based formula that synthesizes an array of factors, or leave the choice up to discretion on a case-by-case basis.

5. *Portfolio construction and allocations*: Once it decides to invest, the team will need to determine the size of the position it wishes to take. It may elect to mirror the composition of an index and replicate the respective weightings of its constituents. It may determine weightings on a discretionary basis, or derive them from a benchmark, a predetermined budget, or some other formula or framework.

6. *Transaction approval and execution*: The decision and action of buying or selling can be made on a team basis or by a single person who signs off on the transaction.

7. *Portfolio adjustments and ongoing trades*: The team may leave the composition of its portfolio static, or periodically adjust its regional, sector, industry, or asset exposures by trimming, enlarging, eliminating, or adding positions. You would need to find out what development would trigger such an adjustment, and what the team's "sell discipline" is.

8. *Risk management*: Many think of investment risk as the probability of losing money and associate it with negative outcomes. But Peter Fisher, a senior advisor to the Systemic Risk Council and former U.S. Treasury official and BlackRock executive, holds a more profound view.

   Fisher defines risk as a deviation from an investment objective, and risk management as an effort to reduce that deviation. "I think it's important to understand risk in these terms," he said in an interview, "because people often lose sight of what their objectives are. They tend to believe that risks are the same for you and me—but they're not, because everyone has different investment objectives. If you're betting that the stock market will go up and I'm betting that it will go down, our objectives and risks are clearly very different." Fisher also refuted the notion that risk is only about adverse outcomes, and characterized it as a fallacy. "The fact is, if you made a lot of money with a certain investment strategy, you also took a lot of risk."[2]

   Investors and their advisors and consultants who look to your firm to behave responsibly will want to learn about its risk-management practices. Encourage the investment team to provide an explanation and include it in your strategy or product profile. The natural home for it is the description of the investment process, to which risk management is germane.

   By what risk-management parameters does the team manage its strategy? For example, does it have a benchmark? If so, what is the portfolio's anticipated tracking error? Does the team rebalance? Does it impose limits on investment concentrations (as a percentage of the total portfolio) in individual holdings, sectors, or regions? Does it hedge its exposure, perhaps through short positions, derivatives, or portfolio overlays? If so, what and how is it hedging? How frequently does the team review and monitor its positions and what subsequent actions does it pursue? How is the team prepared to cope with unforeseen events?

Those are just some of the questions you can pose to your team when inquiring about its risk-management conventions.

(2) Articulating the Investment Process There are two main schools of thought on how to describe a strategy's investment process.

- **Articulation approach #1: A linear sequence**

    Some management teams prefer to frame their process as a linear sequence of discrete steps that begins with a vacant portfolio, as if the team had just put up a shingle, launched its strategy from scratch, and begun searching for its very first investment opportunity under normal market conditions.

    It's a highly effective articulation method for illustrative purposes. Think of it as an animated depiction of an investment opportunity, identified among many others, that is highly appealing. In the evaluation process, it begins gliding down a tapering funnel along with them. The further down it goes, the narrower and more selective the funnel becomes. Less attractive opportunities cannot pass through and are gradually siphoned out. But this opportunity is singular: It manages to survive deeper scrutiny and investigation. With each new qualification satisfied, it continues to course through the thinning corridors of that funnel until it finally makes it to the spout. And then out it goes, to be seized by the management team for investors to profit.

    Rather idyllic, wouldn't you say? Perhaps too idyllic for some people's taste. This method of articulation, in certain respects, describes an investment process *in theory*. Most processes haven't begun with a clean slate since their date of inception, which could have been years ago. In practice, it's likely that the process you describe will have already been running on a portfolio inhabited by previous selections and may follow a slightly different sequence. What's more, investment processes aren't always so neat and tidy like a controlled laboratory experiment—particularly during violent turbulence in the markets or mass investor redemptions.

- **Articulation approach #2: A continuum of activities**

    Other management teams prefer to frame their investment process as a nonlinear (and often circular) continuum of activities going on incessantly, all at once, with no definitive start or finish point. This, too, is a viable articulation method—and perhaps a more realistic mirror of how many portfolios are actually run. Nonetheless, even if you adopt this method, you'll still need to decompose the team's agglomeration of activities into smaller components and explain how each one fits into the larger frame. This breakdown will give investors a mechanical sense of how the team goes about constructing and managing its portfolio.

(It should be noted: Some management teams altogether avoid verbalizing their investment process—whether because they wish to keep it a trade secret, or because they operate haphazardly rather than adhering to a preconceived, systematic, and repeatable discipline that can be expressed as a pattern. If that's the case, then your job as a writer is done before it has even begun.)

Here are two hypothetical examples of investment-process articulation accompanied by illustrations, which you can also include in your profile. The first is framed as a linear sequence, the second as a circular continuum.

INVESTMENT PROCESS EXAMPLE 1 (A LINEAR SEQUENCE)

The management team of InvestorPro's Mid Cap Equity Value strategy follows a disciplined process comprising the following steps (Figure 5.2):

- **Initial screening and company identification:** Using the Global Mid Cap SmartIndex as its benchmark, the team scours a universe of approximately 8,000 companies in 20 developed-market countries with a market capitalization of US$2 to $10 billion. It looks for mid-sized outfits it believes are inadequately covered by sell-side research and may consequently be undervalued.
- **Fundamental analysis:** Upon identifying a select group of 150 to 200 companies worthy of further consideration, the team conducts meticulous analysis to evaluate their management quality, business models, and financial strength. It holds meetings with companies' leadership teams, clients, suppliers, competitors, and investors to determine whether those companies are attractively valued. At this stage, the team establishes a series of metrics to assess each company's valuation, and looks for activities (such as a reorganization or management change) that may serve as catalysts for growth and boost the company's value over the long run.

- **Portfolio construction:** Next, the team selects no more than 60 to 70 companies in which to invest. It assigns a weight to each position that reflects risk/return considerations while remaining within country- and security-specific limits relative to the strategy's benchmark. Lead portfolio manager Holly Headway decides the strategy's country allocations and approves each investment on the basis of impressions from frequent travel, meetings with government officials and company executives, and recommendations by the team's portfolio managers and analysts.

- **Sell discipline:** The team will exit positions in companies that drift from the strategy's permitted market capitalization and/or whose long-term financial prognosis has deteriorated.

- **Risk management:** The team monitors its weightings on a daily basis to ensure they do not exceed a predetermined limit of 15% of the portfolio at cost for country allocation and 8% of the portfolio at cost for security allocation. Additionally, the team adjusts the strategy's risk/return profile periodically to reflect its most current outlook for regional economies and the business fundamentals of individual companies.

FIGURE 5.2 The team's investment process centers on identifying undervalued companies with growth potential

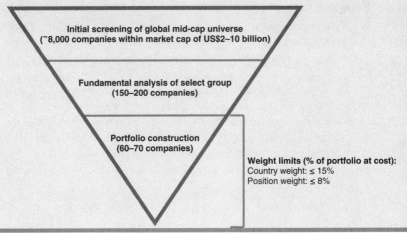

Initial screening of global mid-cap universe
(~8,000 companies within market cap of US$2–10 billion)

Fundamental analysis of select group
(150–200 companies)

Portfolio construction
(60–70 companies)

Weight limits (% of portfolio at cost):
Country weight: ≤ 15%
Position weight: ≤ 8%

INVESTMENT PROCESS EXAMPLE 2 (A CIRCULAR CONTINUUM)

The investment process of InvestorPro's private real estate fund comprises the following components (Figure 5.3):

- **Opportunity sourcing:** The team maintains close consultation with a global network of partner relationships and joint ventures to source deals and access attractive real estate acquisition and development opportunities worldwide. In tapping these connections, the team is able to work with professionals who are intimately familiar with their local real estate markets—and who can support the execution of transactions.

- **Opportunity selection:** The team targets investments in the following three categories for the fund:
  1. Assets divested by governments and corporations
  2. Privately held real estate operating companies that are attractively valued and have growth potential
  3. Commercial and residential real estate developments in target markets

- **Deal execution and property management:** For each of the fund's acquisitions, the team develops and follows a business plan for value creation. After completing an acquisition, it delegates the administration of properties and their daily operation to third-party property managers.

- **Risk management and research:** In an effort to mitigate risks, the team conducts ongoing research, which helps it anticipate the effects of regional developments on the assets it holds—and those it considers acquiring. It continually keeps tabs on key economic and financial parameters (such as interest rates, growth forecasts, employment, and commercial development), as well as local dynamics in the real estate markets in which it invests (e.g., supply and demand, pricing, and capitalization rates). Further, the team harnesses its relationship network to obtain timely, usable information and analysis for making decisions about property acquisitions and sales.

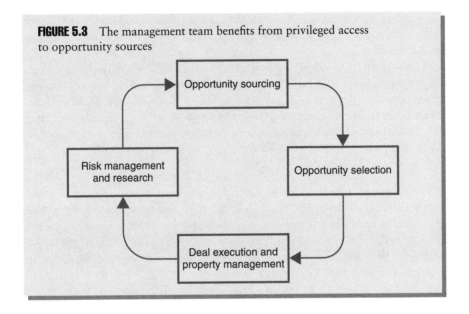

FIGURE 5.3 The management team benefits from privileged access to opportunity sources

Distinguishing Features or Advantages

"Mutato nomine et de te fabula narratur." *(With the name changed, this tale is about you.)*

—Horace

Do you think your firm or investment strategy is so self-evidently special? If your answer is yes, you need not add a section to your profile differentiating its features—though the odds are not in your favor.

In the mid-twentieth century, when one sought to invest through, say, a global strategy, one could only turn to a handful of pioneering managers who set their sights at the horizon, had the vision to leap over geographic boundaries, and offered their clients the ability to pursue opportunities offshore. Today, many types of investment strategies are, at least conceptually, no less commoditized than a quart of milk.

In case you still have your hopes up, here's a humbling exercise: Stack your strategy profile up with those of five leading competitors, and expunge all references to brand names. Then reshuffle the profiles in your deck and have someone read them aloud to you. Can you single yours out? If you can, you're likely in good shape. But if your messages resemble anything you'd find just about anywhere else ("We focus on identifying attractive investment opportunities while managing risks," to cite one example), then your revelation might be difficult to stomach: *Change only the name, and this story is about you.*

Yet plenty of investment firms have attractive distinctions worth highlighting—and not just in strategy or product profiles, but also in RFP responses and pitch books, on your firm's website and social media, and elsewhere. It's often a matter of unearthing them with a journalist's mentality of asking the right questions and bringing out-of-sight information to light. Consider any of the following:

1. **The proof is in the performance.** It's the most prized feat and darling metric any firm could hope to exhibit: If you have a good, long-term track record of performance to prove your distinction, then by all means, do tell. (Short-term performance metrics will shorten the shelf life of your piece and are anyway insufficient to persuade longer-term investors of your strengths.)

2. **The proof is also in the product.** Cite the distinctions of your investment strategy if such exist. One differentiator could be the investment philosophy, as explained in the earlier section of this chapter.

   Firsts are another: Is this strategy the first, or among the first, to foray into an uncharted region or type of asset? Does it provide an unconventional or "one-stop" solution, possess a rare technical feature, have a special blend of characteristics, or follow an uncommon investment process? For example, one European corporate bond strategy claims to integrate "strong qualitative analysis" with "robust quantitative valuation" methods at every stage of the investment process in an effort to identify attractive return opportunities. Another strategy claims to emphasize capital preservation to protect investors during market downturns.

3. **To differentiate, you need to demonstrate.** Always support hackneyed statements with proof points. A nearly ubiquitous assertion of investment firms is that they are "committed to our clients." If you claim you're committed, explain how. Is it through performance-based compensation, which aligns the pay of your management team with client interests? Is it because your portfolio managers co-invest their own money in the fund and have a direct stake in its performance? Is your commitment reflected in any industry awards your firm has earned—whether for performance, client service, or other achievements?

4. **To satisfy, you need to quantify.** Investment firms commonly tout their talent benches, research capabilities, operational staff, and other

strengths. But by assigning numerical values to your resources, you can make them more memorable and tangible. For example, how many offices does your firm have, and in how many regions do you operate? What are your teams' sizes (e.g., number of portfolio managers, analysts, economists, client-service staff, etc.)? Is there any other aspect of your operation you can quantify?

Consider this example of a management team that invests in hedge funds and wishes to impart the scope of its activity ...

Each year, we meet with an average of 130 hedge-fund managers and perform more than 40 due diligence visits. Collectively, our team holds 120 seats on the advisory boards of funds in which we invest.

... or this one, of a management team that invests globally:

The management team draws on a worldwide stable of more than 100 fundamental analysts, 60 quantitative analysts, and 5 economists as of [DATE]. Together, they bring a range of knowledge instrumental for identifying opportunities and constructing portfolios.

On that note, investment organizations that are part of larger financial institutions—such as those that encompass investment banking, trading, and research—would do well to highlight their access to the knowledge, resources, and capabilities of their parent companies.

5. **Sizable operations and administrative staff are a precious advantage.** That's because they free up management teams to focus strictly on running portfolios and serving clients. Dedicated investment resources are a luxury to which not all firms can lay claim, so if you can, state it.

6. **Heritage is an honorable distinction.** There's something to be said for longevity as an enduring testament to success—particularly if there's heritage involved. How long has your firm been in business? Has it pioneered a type of investment strategy, technique, product, or analysis? Has it introduced new ideas or coined terms that have stood the test of time? Is there anything about the firm's operating history that plays an advantageous role in its current strategies on offer? Have the firm's investment offerings been time-tested?

7. **The right relationships are priceless.** Does your firm have privileged access to government officials, the management teams of companies, or circles of industry and academia that allow it to source opportunities, conduct analysis, gain regional insights, exert influence, and cultivate productive relationships with the entities in which it invests?

8. **Organizational structure has its benefits.** In what way is the particular setup of your firm advantageous? Some firms, for example, claim to operate as one unit, not a collection of independent investment-management boutiques. They see cohesion as conducive to teamwork and multilateral sharing of information among colleagues. This cohesion, they say, promotes focus by aligning everyone with common objectives and shared values under one unified culture. It grounds the entire organization to a central core and gives everyone a panoramic view of opportunities and risks across all business lines. When cohesion holds sway, fund managers don't compete to beat each other—they collaborate to help each other, as one firm put it.

   Other firms have equally passionate, valid, and persuasive arguments for the boutique structure. If diversification is what many an investor seeks, what better way to achieve it than through access to a collection of disparate, independent boutiques—each with its own culture, philosophy, and practice? Those firms underscore that investment diversification begins with diversity of thought, opinion, and human organization. It's driven by heterogeneous groups of people. And if those boutiques maintain some cooperation between them and cross-pollinate each other with knowledge and information, all the better.

9. **Local presence, cultural diversity, and genuine expertise are uncommon virtues worth highlighting.** Despite the twenty-first-century ability to conduct business through long-distance communication, there's still merit to commanding a physical presence in target destinations of investment around the globe—or at least to visiting them frequently and basing decisions on firsthand human impressions.

   Valuable, too, are local staff operating in other time zones, or who are versed in the native languages and cultures of their investment regions—assuming they are able to react immediately to market developments, facilitate negotiations and transactions, conduct research, and channel their native understanding of those regions to support investment decisions. One firm points out that members of its global investment team are collectively fluent in more than 20 languages—enough to make even the most cosmopolitan polyglot feel provincial.

   When citing expertise as a differentiator, don't just ascribe it to anyone with an intellectual specialization, however slight. Reserve the term for exceptionally skilled individuals with bona fide credentials—including scholars whose knowledge relates to the investment endeavor. A quant-fund analyst with a doctoral degree in applied mathematics? Check. A managing partner of a fund that invests in oil and natural-gas projects who has a Ph.D. in geology and geophysics? Check. One firm mentioned its work with elder statesmen of the corporate world who are retired executives with experience in the industries targeted by its investment strategies.

10. **Tenure speaks volumes.** If substantial, the longevity of the management team's members can be a strong testament to performance, to their capacity to work effectively together, to their organizational loyalty and dedication, and to the firm's ability to retain them. Here's one example:

> *All portfolio managers have been with the team since its inception. Having worked together for more than 10 years, they offer investors the benefit of their shared experience and successful track record managing investments in X.*

11. **If your proposition sounds commonplace, consider reframing it from the investor's perspective.** Doing so can make it fresher and more appealing. Many firms, for instance, highlight the collaborative approach of their management teams:

> *Our investment decisions are made on a team basis while taking multiple perspectives into account.*

But there's another way to couch this idea that explains how your client would experience the benefit:

> *When investing with our funds, you're not putting your money with a single manager—but rather with a longstanding management team with years of experience and a collective breadth of perspectives.*

12. **Compare and contrast.** It often helps to contrast your firm with the competition by prefacing with what is similar—as a kind of upfront admission that could bolster your credibility—and then sharpening the difference:

> *While alternative investments aren't unique to our business, the legacy and foundations of our franchise are. Those include our multigenerational experience of more than 50 years investing in X, Y, and Z; our talent pool of professionals with knowledge in key areas of the market; and our global capabilities spanning multiple continents—all of which position us to serve our most demanding clients.*

13. Performance may be paramount, but efficiency isn't too far behind.
Although you cannot explicitly or implicitly assure investors of any
profit before it is materialized, what you *can* do is assure them of the
efficiency with which your firm manages their money, assuming your
firm's investment practices can back up that claim.

In a strict, limited sense, an efficient portfolio is either a portfolio
that offers the highest expected return for a given level of risk, or one
with the lowest level of risk for a given expected return. In a broader
sense, to state that your firm manages investments efficiency is to imply
that it conforms to general principles governing efficient portfolio
management:

a. It conceives, designs, and intends for all transactions to be economically appropriate—and carries them out in a cost-effective way.

b. It enters into each transaction for one or more of the following
purposes:

  I. The reduction of risk;

  II. The reduction of cost; and/or

  III. The generation of additional income or capital for the strategy
  with a level of risk that is consistent with the strategy's risk/return
  profile.

For legal reasons, as explained later in Chapter 7, to say that
your firm's portfolio managers "work on generating high returns for
our clients" would be promissory and thus prohibited. However,
if your firm applies the foregoing principles of efficiency, you can
state that "we see to it that our clients' investments are managed
efficiently."

A Description of the Management Team   Apportion a segment of your profile to a brief summary on the team managing the strategy. Who leads it?
What's the total value of assets it manages? You can also list the team's
number of members, as well as a numerical breakdown by function (e.g.,
number of portfolio managers, traders, etc.).

Add a word about the team's talent bench—the nature of members' skills
and functions in aggregate. Are they complementary? Are they broad (meaning that they collectively span multiple areas), deep (meaning that there are
a number of individuals covering each area), or both?

Your summary can address the team as a whole; comprise short, individual biographies of key members; or do both. If you decide to include
biographies, focus them on the individual's current and functional title, job
responsibilities, industry experience, past jobs, and academic and professional credentials. Here's one example:

ABOUT THE GLOBAL ASSET ALLOCATION TEAM

InvestorPro's Global Asset Allocation team manages £23 billion in assets as of [DATE] and consists of 10 investment professionals—including 3 portfolio managers, 5 research analysts, and 2 dedicated traders—averaging 13 years of investment experience.

The team enjoys the benefit of professionals with specialized knowledge in complementary areas that enable it to make informed allocations across equities, fixed income, and alternative assets. Loretta Leader has led the team for 9 years alongside co-managers Paul Partner and Cornelia Comrade. The team is backed by InvestorPro's operational resources, research capabilities, and client-service staff, which enhance its analytical capabilities and allow it to focus exclusively on managing its strategy.

ABOUT LORETTA LEADER

Loretta Leader manages the development and formulation of the firm's asset-allocation strategy, guides the research effort, and participates in the strategy's execution as the lead portfolio manager. Before joining InvestorPro in [YEAR], she was a senior portfolio manager at [FIRM NAME] for [NUMBER OF YEARS] and an analyst at [FIRM NAME] for [NUMBER OF YEARS].

Ms. Leader holds a Chartered Financial Analyst (CFA) designation. She earned an MBA from [SCHOOL NAME] and a BA in [FIELD] from [SCHOOL NAME].

Investment Terms and Parameters at a Glance Consider carving out a section in your strategy or product profile—perhaps in a shaded "call-out" box, or on the left- or right-hand rail—to list key miscellaneous specifications about your offering. It's an effective way of providing time-constrained investors, advisors, and consultants with a cursory view that could help them qualify your proposition more efficiently.

List no more than one or two handfuls of items. (Remember: Your product profile is only the "coming attractions" of an RFP response, discussed later in the RFP section of this chapter, that investors can always turn to for more information.)

Here's a partial list of items to consider for your call-out:

1. Date of strategy or product inception
2. Current assets under management
3. Benchmark
4. Tracking error
5. Target return (typically annual)
6. Type of desired returns (e.g., income, capital appreciation, total returns, absolute returns)
7. The vehicles through which the strategy will be offered (e.g., a U.S. mutual fund or closed-end fund; a European UCITS fund or SICAV; a specialized investment fund, also known as a Luxembourg SIF; a separately managed account; a commingled fund; an Irish collective asset management vehicle, or ICAV; etc.)
8. Share classes offered, if applicable
9. Permitted holdings (i.e., the types of assets targeted by the strategy, such as bonds of a particular credit quality, companies that fall within a certain range of market capitalization, etc.)
10. Geographic mandate (i.e., the regions targeted by the strategy)
11. Minimum investment amount
12. Fee structure
13. Liquidity provisions (i.e., limitations on redemptions and subscriptions, as well as gates), if applicable
14. Typical number of holdings
15. Portfolio turnover (a measure of how long an asset is held on average in the portfolio)
16. Expected and maximum allowable leverage ratios, if applicable
17. Target fund size, which is the amount of capital sought to be raised (typically for private investments)
18. Investment period, commitment period, and term (typically for private investments)
19. The firm's seed commitment to the fund (if applicable) or any co-investments made by the firm alongside its investors
20. Concentration limits (i.e., the maximum percentage of a portfolio that can be allocated to a single holding, sector, region, country, asset class, etc.)
21. Investment style (a general classification of your strategy—such as "long-only," "market-neutral," "value," "growth," "blend," or "low-volatility"—that would help investors, advisors, and consultants place you on the map)

Packaging Your Strategy or Product Profile with Other Literature

Strategy and product profiles of complex, sophisticated offerings—especially those limited to institutional or high-net-worth investors—are typically more descriptive than those intended for a mass retail audience. Consult with the ones who know your constituencies best—your firm's client-facing professionals—to determine whether to limit your profile to the size of a brief one- or two-page fact sheet, or whether to develop a more detailed profile.

Some prefer to include performance (return) history in their profiles. But remember that such information would date your piece and shorten its shelf life. One alternative is to create regularly updated performance fact sheets to be paired with evergreen profiles. Or if you'd like to take the modular approach one step further, consider an à la carte assembly of a kit—perhaps in the form of a pocket folder—that can contain any combination of four elements:

1. A firm overview page
2. A capabilities brochure
3. A profile of the strategy or product to be offered
4. A detailed performance fact sheet to match (which can include key portfolio information)

Such modularity allows for greater packaging flexibility but may not always be efficient or cost-effective. Ultimately, packaging considerations should stem from what your clients expect to receive, how detailed you should be, and what route you believe would produce the most value for the money you spend on content production.

RFP Responses

In some respects, an RFP response (or RFP for short) is a highly detailed version of a strategy or product profile on steroids. It provides the most exhaustive description of virtually all aspects of an investment offering, down to the most technical and administrative. It is framed as a comprehensive reply to the due diligence inquiry of a prospective investor. And it constitutes the firm's official proposal to render investment services.

The Role of Due Diligence Questionnaires Since investor inquiries take the form of long questionnaires and are laborious to answer, consider creating an anticipatory questionnaire for each offering—also known as a due diligence questionnaire (DDQ)—containing stock answers to all the standard questions that investors may pose, and keep those answers on hand for future use. Some firms organize DDQ responses in rationalized databases that facilitate the retrieval of responses to incoming requests.

DDQs will free up your time and resources to focus on idiosyncratic, non-standard queries from specific investors that you might not have anticipated—but that you'll inevitably encounter. You will need that time to provide additional information and craft case-specific responses.

In general, RFP questions vary by the type and nature of the investment strategy they address. Therefore, to compile questions for your DDQ, you'll need to consult with:

- Your firm's product managers, portfolio managers, traders, analysts, and research professionals, who are versed in the mechanics of the strategy at hand
- Your sales staff, who have a good sense of what prospective investors tend to inquire about
- Industry associations, which can provide information on the investor's due-diligence process

Here is just a small sample of common questions to expect. (For more on how to answer some of them, refer to the previous section of this chapter on strategy and product profiles.)

1. **The firm**
   a. Describe your firm's organizational structure, geographic locations, and lines of business, including those unrelated to the investment strategy offered herein.
   b. Provide a history of your firm, including past mergers and acquisitions, if applicable.
   c. Is the firm a publicly held company? If so, on what exchanges does it trade?
   d. List all affiliations, directorships, and memberships of the company and its principals.
2. **The investment management team**
   a. Describe the structure of your team and include an organizational chart depicting each member.
   b. Provide a biography of each team member that includes current title and job description; years of professional experience; years served at the firm; previously held jobs; academic credentials; and industry certifications and designations.

    c. How do you handle key-person risk? Indicate whether you have a succession plan that addresses the departure of team members, describe it, and list your staff turnover for the past 5 years.

    d. How are the team members' compensation aligned with investors' interests? Do you provide performance-based compensation?

3. The investment strategy

    a. Describe the investment objective, philosophy, and process of your strategy.

    b. Detail any changes your strategy has undergone over the past 5 years.

    c. Describe your risk-management procedures and policies for the strategy in the context of corporate governance. Clarify whether your firm has a separate team with independent jurisdiction to manage risks and enforce decisions.

4. Research, analysis, and evaluation

    a. Discuss your methods and process for conducting research while describing the internal and external resources at your disposal for obtaining intelligence.

    b. What valuation methods do you employ for assessing investment opportunities?

    c. How many investment opportunities do you review annually?

5. Performance, fees, and administration

    a. Describe your performance history, and explain how the team managed past episodes of underperformance or challenging market conditions.

    b. Specify your fee structure, including performance-based fees and management fees.

    c. Describe your client-reporting conventions, including format, frequency, and detail.

    d. What activities do you subcontract to outside agents?

Editorial Guidelines for RFPs Pity those poor, neglected RFPs: They're often tucked away in the backyard of firms' marketing operations and regarded as the unsightly stepchildren of investment literature. Though unjustifiable, this treatment is to be expected.

RFPs are, to put it tactfully, less-than-glamorous documents. They are storehouses of detail, molded in formulaic, cut-and-dried fashion as dictated by the inquirer's line of questioning. They don't lend themselves to much content curation or mold-breaking imagination. They are laden with text and routinely low on graphics. No wonder they take a backseat to their glossy, snazzy brochure brethren. But they shouldn't.

Considering RFPs' pivotal role in the client's due diligence and in the investment firm's bid for clinching a deal, it's surprising to witness how many of them suffer from poor editorial standards. RFPs ought to be treated as premier literature in their own right since they link directly to the sales process. In fact, oftentimes they're the first to be requested in bidding solicitations—especially by institutional investors—which puts them very much on the frontline of communication. Yet, if to judge by their commonly inferior writing and production quality, they are seldom paid their due and insufficiently viewed as an opportunity for a firm to put its best foot forward. At worst, a substandard RFP can squander a mandate or demote an investment firm in the view of prospective investors and consultants.

What makes for a strong RFP? It a nutshell, it should be:

- **Accessible,** which is to say reader-friendly
- **A more compelling read than a typical pro forma questionnaire or drab repository of information,** which is how many firms treat it—at their peril
- **A communication vehicle for differentiating your firm,** as RFPs aren't just a platform for spotlighting your investment advantages—but also a terrific opportunity to stand out in the way you articulate your responses, substantiate your assertions, and telegraph the particulars of your offering

The following are some editorial guidelines to consider.

1. Preface your RFP with an executive summary.

Not only will your typical RFP be several pages long; it will also be only one of several RFPs by a host of bidders that the investor will need to review. That's a lot of reading, so show mercy upon your audience.

Why not have your RFP stand out in the pile with a succinct overview in the beginning highlighting all your essential points? The summary should be no more than two pages long, reflect what the prospective client most needs to know, or simply display the highlights of your strategy or product profile. Among the useful points to include:

- The strategy's definition and philosophy
- A brief description of the investment process—or at least the investment universe, your selection qualifications, and your typical portfolio size
- A summary of terms, including available vehicles and their inception date, the minimum investment required, fees, subscription information, and redemption constraints
- A word about your risk-management discipline

- ■ Distinguishing characteristics
- ■ A short paragraph about the management team

2. **Use visual enhancements.**

They help ease the reading experience and make your RFP more digestible and optically appealing. Employ bullets and subheads to break up long passages of text. (Refer to the previous section on strategy and product profiles for two examples of investment-process articulation as a demonstration of this concept.) Consider incorporating shaded boxes of text to emphasize key points or highlight certain messages.

Use graphics. Accompany your explanations with charts and illustrations—as you would in a brochure or a research paper—and don't forget to number and title each exhibit and couple it with a reference it in the text. For instance, the title of an illustration could be: "Table 5.4: The fund's investment process consists of five stages." The text would then read: "The fund follows a due diligence process, as illustrated in Table 5.4."

3. **Follow the previously mentioned guidelines for describing your firm and its offerings.**

Refer to the earlier sections of this chapter for an overview of how to explain your organization and its capabilities; its strategies, products, and management teams; and its differentiating qualities.

4. **Don't attempt to say too much in one breath.**

The so-called "loaded question"—the kind that elicits a heavily detailed answer—has a tendency to provoke respondents to cram as much information as they can in prohibitively long sentences. Avoid that snare.

If you find yourself having to give lengthy answers, break them up into serial components and consider listing them as bulleted particulars. You can also take the string of ideas you wish to convey and divide it into appositional components that logically dovetail with each other, such as "problem" with "solution," "cause" with "consequence," "condition" with "result," or "before" with "after."

For example, when asked about its approach to an equity strategy, one firm replied like so:

> *The management team aims to avoid paying too much for stocks by emphasizing cash flow instead of reported earnings in order to identify discounted opportunities with attractive long-term potential while neutralizing various accounting assumptions that may variably affect earnings results.*

Whew! Did you get that?

Now consider dividing that statement into three components: the problem (the susceptibility of earnings to accounting manipulations); the proposed solution (looking at cash flow); and the result (investing in discounted companies for less). What you get is the following:

> *In the team's view, earnings results are an inaccurate indicator of a company's valuation, because they are more highly susceptible to accounting manipulations than cash flow.*
>
> *Thus, when analyzing stocks in which to invest, the team emphasizes cash-flow valuations—rather than reporting earnings—in an effort to:*
>
> - *Identify discounted companies with attractive, long-term potential; and*
> - *Avoid overpaying for their stock.*

5. Maintain focus in your answers.

Have you begun answering the question within the first five to seven words of your response? If not, you've lost focus and risk annoying your reader and undermining your bidding effort.

One way to focus your answer is to echo the question in your opening:

Question: How do you source investment opportunities?

Answer: We source investment opportunities by ...

Question: What is your strategy's investment objective?

Answer: Our strategy's investment objective is to ...

Don't give roundabout answers, even if the question is delicate or uncomfortable. Your reader needs to know the answer one way or another, so you'd rather provide it head-on and then add context if you need to. If you're digressive or defensive in the very opening of your answer, it will show, and give rise to suspicion.

Suppose, for example, that you're asked to describe turnover among the portfolio-management team, and your turnover is unflatteringly high. Don't play for time and beat around the bush. Be upfront. You can open with a table listing all the individuals your firm has gained and lost over the period specified in the question. You can then provide color by highlighting your tenured members, by clarifying whether the turnover actually had any effect on the business, and by detailing your succession plan, assuming you have one.

When asked a yes/no question (e.g., "Do you ever share fees with third parties or consultants?"), don't leave your readers hanging for too long to find out the ultimate "yes" or "no" answer, even if you'd like to infuse your response with context. Begin upfront with variations of the following:

- Yes
- No
- That depends on … [immediately followed by when "yes" and/or "no"]
- Yes, with the exception of …
- No, with the exception of …
- Yes, however …
- Usually/typically/mostly yes, however …
- No, however …
- Usually/typically/mostly no, however …

6. **Write with economy.**

Longer is better only to expound on an idea. But whenever possible, play the minimalist chef and trim, trim, trim your word count. Even a small reduction in each answer can add up and go a long way in a 40-plus question RFP.

Focus on trimming answers to perfunctory questions that merely serve the inquirer's checkbox, and wield the ax on superfluous words.

Example #1: When an unnamed firm was asked whether it was regulated by the Financial Services Authority in the U.K., it replied with 17 words ("Yes, we can confirm that our organization is regulated by the Financial Services Authority in the U.K."), whereas just eight words would have sufficed ("Yes, we are regulated by the U.K.'s F.S.A."). That's less than half the word count.

Example #2: Another firm was asked about the format and frequency of its holdings statements. It responded with 44 words …

> *We can provide holdings statements throughout the month for our clients. We provide these statements in either Excel or PDF format. We provide these statements from as early as the fifth business day of the month through the twelfth, as best suits the client.*

… that could have been trimmed down to 27:

> *We can provide holdings statements in either Excel or PDF format—from the 5th business day of the month through the 12th—as best suits the client.*

7. Justify fees in terms of costs.

The investment firm Invesco conducted a study some years ago on how language describing investment products resonated with clients, and found that using "costs" rather than "fees" can make a big difference in how people perceive being charged for their investments.[3]

According to the study, "fee" had the most negative connotation—perhaps because it implies a more opportunistic way of charging—whereas "cost" triggered the most positive association. (Somewhere in between were "charges" and "commissions.") Intuitively, this makes sense: "Cost" and "charge" are corollaries to the value of a service and thus tend to justify themselves.

This is not to imply that you should play the spin doctor and altogether avoid using the (other) F-word. "Fee" is, after all, the most widely associated word with terms of payment—one that many investors have come to expect when they use it in their RFP questions. But "costs" and "charges" are words to consider when expounding on how your firm expects to be remunerated for its services.

For example, some RFPs may ask whether your firm's fees are negotiable. One way to respond, assuming you feel that you have justifiably answered "no," is to defend the fee as a fair reflection of the *cost* and *value* of your service.

8. Aim for consistency.

If an RFP is to share a perch with other foundational literature, then it should share consistent messaging on all matters organizational and product-related. Consistency breeds reinforcement, and RFPs are no exception.

Following these guidelines should do your RFPs justice in an effort to win mandates.

Pitch Books

A pitch book is a marketing presentation, typically in PowerPoint format, containing key highlights of an investment offering. Think of it as a presentation version of a strategy or product profile, or an abridged proposal.

More broadly, pitch books are messaging decks containing the latest information on the firm's strategies, products, and services. You can produce and use them as up-to-date sources of reference—both internally for firm colleagues and externally for clients. You can use them as handouts, not just as presentations. And since each pitch book is a modular document, you can elect to share just portions of it containing select pages (or slides) of interest.

Editorial Guidelines for Pitch Books Since pitch books take the form of a presentation, you don't need to write them in fully formed prose or complete sentences. A telegraphic style—as demonstrated in the section titled "Setting the Appropriate Style" in Chapter 4—would do, meaning that you may omit nonessential words, such as certain modal and auxiliary verbs, prepositions, conjunctions, and descriptors. One suggested format is to write each page as a list of points in shorthand encapsulating key messages.

Also, when it comes to pitch books, think "picture books": Have images, diagrams, and charts animate your points as you would in any presentation. For example, you can use organizational charts to sketch out your firm's structure or investment teams, flowcharts to portray the investment process, graphs to depict numerical information, and associative imagery (such as photographs or illustrations).

How should you structure your pitch book? There is no single convention, but you can adopt variations of the following sequence:

- A cover page (slide #1) and table of contents (slide #2)
- Legal disclaimers and an overview of risk factors to consider in the investment offering
- Part #1: A distilled overview of the investment offering and/or introductory explanation of the opportunity involved (this part can include a broad definition of your offering and its aim, and perhaps one or two distinguishing characteristics)
- Part #2: The reasons to choose your firm (as explained in the previous section on strategy and product profiles)
- Part #3: An in-depth review of the offering and/or opportunity (this section can include research or general observations that make the case for your strategy; a description of your strategy's objectives, philosophy, and process; and a summary of investment terms—all of which are explained in the section on strategy and product profiles)
- Part #4: An overview of the investment management team, including the team's structure and members' biographies
- Part #5: The strategy's or fund's performance history, if applicable
- Part #6: A conclusion summarizing key takeaway points
- An appendix containing addendums you wish to relegate as references to the very end (such as a glossary of terms, an elaboration on certain technical points or sources of research)

A Hypothetical Example   Suppose the fictitious firm InvestorPro is offering a private fund—let's call it the "InvestorPro Groundwork Partners" fund—to invest in infrastructure. Here's an example of how three slides of its pitch book might read (Figures 5.4, 5.5 and 5.6):

FIGURE 5.4   An Overview of the Investment Offering

> **InvestorPro Groundwork Partners: Opportunity Overview**
>
> • A private fund that will invest in equity interests of infrastructure assets in Australia and New Zealand
>
> • Target sectors: transportation, energy and utilities, social infrastructure and communication
>
> • Majority of returns to be achieved through cash-generative assets
>
> • Attractive risk/return profile:
>   • Conservatively moderate leverage
>   • Stable, predictable cash flows
>   • A gross internal-rate-of-return (IRR) target of 12 to 15%
>
> • Seasoned professionals with rich experience in infrastructure, private-equity, and real-estate investing
>
> • Fundraising target: AU$5 billion

FIGURE 5.5   The Fund's Target Investments

Infrastructure Assets Targeted by the Fund

Transportation

• Toll roads
• Bridges
• Tunnels
• Airports
• Rail and mass transit networks
• Parking facilities

Social infrastructure

• Educational facilities
• Healthcare facilities

Energy and utilities

• Water distribution and treatment facilities
• Oil and gas pipelines
• Power plants

Communications

• Cable networks
• Cell towers
• Satellite networks

FIGURE 5.6 An Overview of Investment Benefits

The Benefits of Infrastructure Assets

- Essential for functioning societies and economies

- Have long, useful lives

- Monopolistic or exhibit high barriers to entry

- Generally immune to shifts in the business cycle

- Generate steady streams of income that is often correlated with inflation

---

Case Studies

Case studies showcase practical applications of your firm's investment ideas, strategies, and solutions. They can exhibit a proof of concept, explain how a plan was put to use, demonstrate the advantages of pursuing a course of action, chronicle the practice of a method or process, or highlight a success story.

Examples of Case Study Topics Consider the following examples of what actual firms have done:

1. **The benefits of certain types of assets:** To illustrate the return and diversification benefits of real assets (such as real estate, commodities, and agricultural land), one firm published a case study showing how an insurance company invested in such assets to support its annuity products.
2. **A problem-solving strategy:** Another firm issued a case study on how it sought to help a corporate retirement-plan sponsor achieve a surplus of assets in excess of its liabilities through a complex strategy of risk management and return generation.
3. **A process "in action":** One firm developed a case study chronicling the due-diligence investigations it conducts to evaluate securities denominated in local currencies of offshore markets before investing in them. The purpose of this written account is to demonstrate the firm's research capabilities, analytical rigor, and deft management of risks.

How to Formulate a Case Study The way you choose to formulate a case study depends on the subject. Is it a solution to a problem, a proof of concept, a detailed account of a process, a success story—or perhaps a combination of the four? As in the case of other types of investment literature, no single formula fits all.

Here is one suggested outline of components that could work for describing a problem/solution scenario:

Part #1: An overview of the client's problem

Part #2: The solution put forth by the investment firm for consideration

Part #3: The strategy formulated and proposed

Part #4: The strategy's implementation

Part #5: The measures by which success was defined—and the results

Part #6: A takeaway conclusion

An Example of Case Study Writing Drawing on example #1 of the case study topics mentioned earlier, suppose the make-believe firm InvestorPro offered one of its institutional clients—an insurance company called InsuranceTrust—a custom-tailored investment strategy designed to help fund the company's annuity obligations. InsuranceTrust decided to tap InvestorPro for its service and, thanks to the strategy, has so far been able to meet its commitments.

Now, InvestorPro wants to issue a case study that would demonstrate its success to other clients. Here's a hypothetical example—written simplistically just for illustrative purposes—of how a summarized version could be written:

Case Study: Putting Real Assets to Work in Support of Annuity Products

Like other insurance companies, InsuranceTrust maintains a general account (GA), which contains a pool of capital made available to pay claims and benefits to which policyholders are entitled. In particular, the GA backs InsuranceTrust's ability to fund payments to annuity policyholders.

The GA draws its capital from two sources in order to help fund those payments:

- Contributions made by policyholders
- The growth of its assets through investing

1. **InsuranceTrust's challenge**

   Since policyholders' contributions to the GA do not produce nearly enough capital for InsuranceTrust to make future annuity payments, the GA relies heavily on proceeds generated by investing its assets. These proceeds constitute a significant portion of its funding. Therefore, the GA's investment strategy needs to produce attractive returns.

At the same time, the strategy should emphasize stable returns and low volatility so as not to expose the GA's capital to undue risk that could result in prohibitive losses. That's because InsuranceTrust is obligated to provide a minimum payment of principal and interest to all of its policyholders—and its GA must meet statutory funding requirements to support this obligation (Figure 5.7).

2. The solution put forth for consideration

Following a comprehensive study of InsuranceTrust's assets, current liabilities, and future obligations, InvestorPro proposed incorporating three types of real assets into the GA's portfolio: real estate, agricultural land, and energy commodities, such as oil and natural gas. (The first two were pursued through direct private investments, and the third through futures contracts.)

According to InvestorPro's research, these assets could help the GA match its current assets against current and future funding liabilities: They offer the potential for attractive current income, long-term capital appreciation as a hedge against inflation, and low correlations with traditional assets (such as stocks and bonds) that might curb risks.

3. The strategy

InvestorPro conducted further analysis and devised the following allocation strategy for the GA's assets (Figure 5.8):

- Cash: 30%
- Short-term fixed income: 25%
- Energy commodities: 20%
- Commercial real estate: 15%
- Agricultural land: 10%

FIGURE 5.7 InsuranceTrust's general account uses proceeds from its investments to fund payments to annuity policyholders

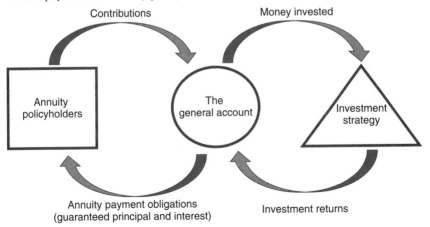

FIGURE 5.8   InvestorPro's allocation strategy was intended to help InsuranceTrust balance assets with liabilities

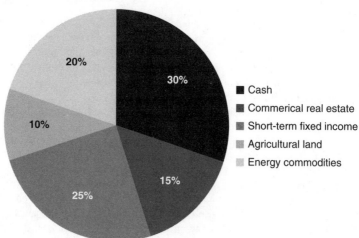

The proposed allocation was designed to provide attractive income, moderate capital appreciation with limited risk, and sufficient liquidity to meet current obligations. Given InsuranceTrust's need to maintain a conservative risk profile, InvestorPro assigned the greatest allocations to the most liquid assets.

4. Execution

To pursue its proposed allocation, InvestorPro assumed the management of InsuranceTrust's GA assets through a separately managed account while enlisting the management teams of its real-asset strategies to construct the portfolio and monitor risks.

InvestorPro also sourced and identified opportunities for direct private investments in agricultural land through its network of relationships with property owners.

5. Results

Five years later, InvestorPro has been able to report the following:

a. Attractive risk/return characteristics

The GA has achieved moderate but steady levels of income, capital appreciation, and effective diversification, which have served as a cushion against inflation and episodic volatility.

b. Advantages to private, long-term access

Thanks to direct private ownership of agricultural land, the GA was able to generate accretive income from leasing, which provided insulation from short-term spates of volatility in commodity pricing. Additionally, the GA has enjoyed increased flexibility in managing its long-term investments, since real assets (unlike bonds) do not mature on a given schedule. Rather, they enable investors to hold them indefinitely, sell them, or reinvest in them, as needed.

c. The benefit of commodity holdings

The GA has benefited from exposure to the global commodities market, which offset a cyclical contraction in demand for agricultural products in the United States during part of the year.

The Packaging and Use of Case Studies Keep four things in mind for case studies:

1. **Apply discretion to packaging.** You can package your case study as a paper, brochure, or pamphlet, depending on how long it is, how you see fit to lay it out, and what visual and graphic elements you wish to incorporate.
2. **Case studies tend to be institutionally focused.** They typically describe complex instances involving organizational subjects rather than individuals, and many investment firms use them primarily for institutional investors and their consultants.
3. **You may not be able to cite clients' names in your study.** That's because many prefer to remain anonymous so as not to reveal sensitive aspects of their internal finances, challenges, and strategies. Be prepared to write your study on a nameless basis if you need to.
4. **Case studies are optional.** Unlike other essential types of foundational literature—such as strategy profiles, RFPs, capability brochures, and pitch books—case studies usually aren't required by investors evaluating your offerings. But they can serve as a powerful testament of your capabilities and validate your credibility if you're able to provide them.

Topical Brochures

Whereas firm-overview and capability brochures advertise functional capacity—the firm's reservoirs of knowledge and skill, its technical proficiency, its strategic disciplines, and operational resources—topical brochures discuss the broader purpose. They convey the firm's instrumental role in bringing investment ideas to life and helping clients achieve their financial goals.

If the words *retirement brochure* ring familiar, you might have already seen one—possibly with a cover image of a mature couple walking hand in hand along a beachfront. (Clichés aside, Arianna Huffington, president and editor-in-chief of Huffington Post Media Group, challenged the outdated notion of retirement as merely the end of a long career, and introduced a more holistic way of thinking about the possibilities latent in people's advanced years as they enter new acts in life.[4] "Can we retire the word 'retirement'?" she pleaded in her thought-provoking remarks at a J.P. Morgan retirement symposium. "It comes from the French word for 'withdraw,' and that's not how people see their later years."[5] Something to think about as you compose messages for your next "investing for retirement" brochure, perhaps?)

Topical brochures usually come in two flavors:

1. **Objective-driven:** Brochures covering familiar aims, such as investing to finance the cost of education (or, dare we say, retirement)
2. **Thematic:** Brochures presenting "big ideas" that cut across investment disciplines, such as opportunities to monetize social and technological trends pervading the world.

Let's explore one example for each.

Example #1 (Objective-Driven): A Brochure on Investing to Finance the Cost of Education Imagine that the pretend firm InvestorPro is offering a tax-advantaged savings plan to finance the college tuition of a loved one. To market the plan, InvestorPro is developing a brochure on investing for education. Here's a rough outline of messages and exhibits such a brochure could include. (Note that some of the figures in this example are inaccurate and meant solely for illustrative purposes.)

- **Part #1: The challenge**
  A college education is highly advantageous in today's competitive world, with college graduates earning X percent more on average than non-graduates. But without prior financial preparation, the cost of a higher education can be prohibitive.
- **Part #2: Establishing a goal**
  It's vital to determine what a college education would cost—and how much you may need to invest toward financing it. Here you will find a table, based on research, listing the projected cost of college and estimated monthly investment for four years of public school and four years of private school according to your beneficiary's age today. The table assumes an average annual increase of 5 percent in college costs (Table 5.4).
- **Part #3: The benefits of a tax-advantaged savings plan**
  InvestorPro's government-accredited, tax-advantaged savings plan for college enables your investments to grow free from federal income taxes. Consider a hypothetical, one-time investment of US$15,000 with

TABLE 5.4 Assessing your future tuition expenses

Child's age (years)	4 years of public school		4 years of private school	
	Projected college cost	Estimated monthly investment	Projected college cost	Estimated monthly investment
Newborn	$X	$Y	$A	$B
1				
2				
3 and so on …				

an X percent annual rate of return in a tax-free account versus an identical investment in a taxable account (Figure 5.9).

- **Part #4: The specific advantages of InvestorPro's savings plan**
  InvestorPro's college-savings plan offers you an efficient, flexible way to invest for college in the following respects:
  1. It allows you to use assets to pay for qualified expenses at any accredited institution of higher education.
  2. It imposes no income limits that restrict participation.
  3. You can choose and change the beneficiaries of this plan—and withdraw funds—at any time.

FIGURE 5.9 A tax-advantaged account can boost potential returns

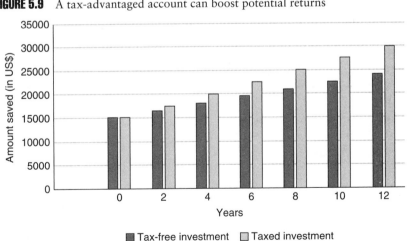

4. You can invest as little as $100 to open an account.

5. Through our plan, you will gain access to InvestorPro's variety of investment strategies managed by experienced teams across multiple disciplines.

- **Part #5: Selecting the investment strategy that is right for you**
  InvestorPro offers three types of portfolio allocations:
  1. A conservative portfolio that emphasizes capital preservation and may be appropriate for older beneficiaries approaching college age and/or for more risk-averse investors
  2. A balanced portfolio with moderate risk that provides a medium between principal safety and capital growth
  3. An aggressive portfolio invested in higher-risk, higher-return opportunities—and designed for very young beneficiaries with long investment horizons

Example #2 (Thematic): A Brochure on Monetizing Global Trends This time, InvestorPro is developing a thematic brochure titled "Monetizing Tomorrow's Trends." The brochure discusses global trends that, according to the firm, present investment opportunities for handsome returns in the medium and long term. Consider the following outline:

- **Part #1: The global trends we find compelling**
  As long-term investors, we at InvestorPro seek to identify opportunities associated with salient trends around the world.

  Today we recognize a number of trends that we believe will affect the planet on which we live, revolutionize healthcare, and harness the benefits of a global economy. These trends concern three key areas in which we see promising possibilities for investors:
  - Climate change
  - Genomic medicine
  - Information technology
- **Part #2: The investment potential**
  1. **Climate change**
     Shifts in global weather patterns pose a variety of threats—from droughts and rising sea levels to violent storms—that are prompting governments and corporations to address climate issues stemming from man-made causes. For example, countries in both hemispheres have enacted regulatory measures to curb greenhouse-gas emissions.

And support continues to grow for the exploration and production of renewable energy that harnesses such sources as solar power and hydropower.

We see investment opportunities in a variety of industries—from energy to automobile manufacturing—that are positioned to comport with new regulatory regimes and help energy consumers reduce their environmental footprint.

2. Genomic medicine

Advancements in decoding the human genome—the sequence of compounds that make up the DNA in human cells—have ushered in the prospect of breakthroughs in medicine. Cheaper and more rapid decoding methods may help medical facilities and drug manufacturers predict one's diseases; tailor medications to one's specific needs; cure terminal illnesses; and greatly increase life expectancy.

InvestorPro pursues investments in businesses and institutions that stand to prosper from progress in genomic medicine by delivering more effective cures—and ultimately revolutionizing healthcare as we know it.

3. Information technology

In this era of cloud computing and handheld devices, hundreds of millions of people take photographs, produce videos, send e-mail and text messages, and store massive volumes of data flooding networks and servers each day. According to one study by [NAME OF RESEARCH INSTITUTE], the past two years alone have generated most of the world's data.

Companies that develop the infrastructure for data transmission, collection, and storage may be poised to profit from the growing deluge of data being disseminated the world over. We also pursue investments in companies that specialize in organizing and analyzing vast amounts of data. Such companies could thrive financially on their ability to discern large-scale trends, glean valuable business intelligence, and offer their findings to corporations, governments, and research institutes.

▪ **Part #3: The connection to InvestorPro's strategies**

InvestorPro's suite of funds is led by our experienced portfolio managers, who aim to monetize global trends by investing in equity and debt of businesses that find new ways to meet society's evolving needs.

We favor companies with forward-thinking management; innovative products that are disrupting industries; and business models adaptable to change, with the capacity to generate solid profits.

Concluding Foundational Literature with a Call to Action

Don't forget to cap your foundational literature—whether it's a brochure, product profile, or pitch book—with an encouragement for investors to reach out to your firm or an intermediary and pursue a dialogue.

Here's one example:

> *For more information about X, visit www.investorpro.com, contact your financial advisor, or set up a meeting with one of our investment professionals available at [PHONE NUMBER and/or E-MAIL ADDRESS].*

PART 2: INTELLECTUAL CAPITAL

capital \ ˈkapədl \ noun
—[with modifier:] a valuable resource of a particular kind.

Join in, fellow writers, for this type of non-monetary capital falls squarely under your domain of responsibility. Broadly defined, intellectual capital is a body of literature containing the collective knowledge and viewpoints of a firm's investment professionals.

What topics does such literature cover? Investments, business and the financial markets, of course, but also myriad other affairs—current and historical, global and domestic, economic and political, environmental and social—that concern your firm's investment strategies and holdings. Is there a forthcoming election somewhere in the world that could have economic consequences? Social unrest threatening to disrupt a political order and impact markets? A natural disaster, health crisis, or impending government policy that could affect the business climate of a region? How about a positive development, such as the establishment of diplomatic relations, a peace treaty, or a trade agreement between countries that could open doors of opportunity? Prepare to ventriloquize your firm's research, analysis, and opinions on the subject, and ready your keyboard to spell out the ramifications for investors.

In addition to matters of public interest, intellectual capital can cover any trade or area of commerce, research, development, or exploration with which your firm's investments intersect. Examples include science, technology, medicine, food, retail, media, telecommunication, housing, energy, transportation … and the list goes on. (Even the arts cross paths with investing. Moviemakers, for instance, have turned to investment banks for film financing. One investment fund that launched in 2016 was designed to finance music-concert tours and album production. And visual art, widely appreciated for its aesthetic pleasure and human expression, is viewed by some firms through the lens of portfolio management as a financial asset that can offer economic benefits.)

Suppose, for example, that your firm offers a fund that invests, among its many holdings, in two companies. One develops 3-D printers that can produce human tissue at a molecular level. The other is engineering a new type of material that would extend the life of lithium batteries (the kind used in portable electronics) by allowing electrons to flow more freely. Perhaps an introductory paper on nanotechnology—the field those two companies share in common—would be in order. Written in plain, accessible terms, such a paper could help demystify the topic for your clients and provide educational context for the value and purpose of their investment in your fund.

The Strategic Use of Intellectual Capital

At its finest, investing is a venture of polymaths and horizon gazers who take great pains to study, analyze, interpret, form opinions on, respond to, and assume stakes in a panorama of disparate things going on in the world. It's what makes developing intellectual capital such a nourishing and absorbing experience for a writer: to learn from knowledgeable professionals, help them author written work about varied subjects, and educate the investor.

Getting paid to learn, write, and instruct is a worthy occupation and a privileged one at that. Yet intellectual capital serves more than just to edify. Writers should be aware of its dual aim: yes, to purvey knowledge—but also to market their firm. Investing is a business after all.

There's nothing illegitimate about the marketing purpose of intellectual capital so long as it is backed by, and harmonized with, intellectual integrity. Here's another way to put it: Intellectual capital isn't meant for sheer exposition. It can and should be deployed strategically as a marketing tool in the service of an enterprise—but always on the basis of sound research, grounded opinions that aren't manipulated to be self-serving, and a perceived tangible benefit for investors.

Consider these pointers:

1. **Cover topics that relate to your firm's offerings or resonate with investors, advisors, and consultants.**

   Investment firms have no business justification running general-interest publications, so be strategic in your choice of topic.

   How about a paper on, say, meteorology? It would make strategic sense if you couched it as an investment-related matter and were able to associate it with—for instance—your catastrophe-bond fund. You could then explore the topic at length, perhaps as part of a campaign to educate investors about the financial perils associated with weather phenomena; about climate vocabulary—from typhoons and cyclones to hurricanes; about the role of catastrophe bonds as a form of capital-markets insurance against losses from natural disasters; and about the potential benefits from investing in such bonds.

   Yet not every topic needs to be tied to your offerings or sales effort. There are plenty of matters that permeate various aspects of society—social trends, lifestyles, business, technology—and that investors and their advisors find informative as participants with stakes in the financial markets. Papers on such topics, along with your firm's viewpoint on them, would not only touch an interested audience but also expand your reader base as recipients share your literature with others. It's called free marketing.

   As of this writing, simultaneous revolutions are going in such areas as retail (which is being reconfigured by e-commerce); cryptocurrencies (with the advent of blockchain); artificial intelligence; and machine learning. These are just some of the many topics you can write about, assuming your firm can provide original perspectives or research on them.

   Remember that intellectual capital—even the kind associated with your firm's offerings—shouldn't be used for sales propositions, as explained next.

2. **Don't conflate intellectual capital with foundational literature.**

   The latter (explained in the previous section on foundational literature) concerns itself solely with the features of your firm's business, their explicit advertisement, and the way they are distinguished from competitors.

Intellectual capital, on the other hand, commands the academic rather than promotional sphere of the communication effort. It's the province of empirical observations, inquiry, and discovery; of independent thought and investigation; of rigorous case building and proof points. It serves to showcase your firm's research, knowledge, and intellectual prowess toward helping investors explore possibilities and achieve their objectives. It is also a communication asset—one too precious to be muddled by a sales pitch. Make every effort to keep it product-agnostic lest you diminish its credibility.

If you'd like to use intellectual capital to make the general case for investing in, say, renewable energy, that's fine. But don't use it as a platform for touting your energy fund. That's what foundational literature is for.

The difference can be summed up like this:

Foundational literature is about positioning yourself.

Intellectual capital is about taking a position.

Which brings us to the next pointer.

3. **Candid viewpoints will help protect one of your firm's most critical assets.**

Oftentimes, investment managers will need to opine on market developments in a way that may not necessarily win them new clients—at least not in the near term. But they are better off expressing their opinions with candor if they wish to maintain their reputation as a credible authority—a prized asset by every measure in the investment business.

In January 2016, when the equity markets were tumbling on worries about China's decelerating economy, the CEO of a large firm said he believed there wasn't "enough blood on the street"—implying that he expected stocks to drop further—even though equity funds are a major chunk of his business. (As a colleague once said, if you're always bullish on everything, the bears will rip your street cred apart.)

The year before, one chief investment officer pointed out in a blog that his prediction about the movement of a particular currency—a forecast he had made on the basis of economic trends he was observing—was wrong.

Another CIO used to publish a bucket list of market prognostications at the beginning of each year, and would then score himself how accurate they turned out by year's end.

Those are just some among many instances of well-chronicled integrity in the annals of investment commentary.

4. **In your approach to writing intellectual capital, think "conversation starter."**

Laurence Sterne, an eighteenth-century novelist, once remarked that "writing, when properly managed [...] is but a different name for a conversation." If it's true for writing in general, it's doubly true for the type of investment literature that, quite literally, gets conversations going between investors and those who serve them.

Firms' client-facing professionals—account managers, sales staff, and others—often use intellectual capital as a catalyst for igniting discussions with their constituencies.

A conversation can be triggered by a market event, positive or negative, on which a firm would publish a paper detailing its analysis and observations. The firm could then use the paper as an occasion to reach out to the investor, discuss the potential consequences or opportunities for the investor's portfolio, and follow up with foundational literature to explore ways in which it could assist the investor through its offerings.

Not all conversations are event-driven. For example, a firm may use a primer you've written on a particular subject as context for outreach and a preliminary dialogue about an investment topic. As the discussion narrows down to specifics, the firm would then turn to foundational literature to exhibit its associated products and technical capabilities.

Intellectual capital and foundational literature have a symbiotic relationship—the former as a display of ideas, the latter as their translation to products and execution—with each being activated at alternate phases of the firm's interactions with investors.

5. **When it comes to current events, focus on your firm's interpretation of what they mean for the investor.**

Did something just happen in some corner of the globe that could bear implications for your investors? It is your duty to communicate to them. But intellectual capital is *not* journalism per se—nor is journalism a field many investment firms wish to claim. A newsroom requires dedicated resources and constitutes a business unto its own. Besides, for a comprehensive account of the news, investors can always turn to the media as a source.

Unless your firm has a bit of news no other reporter can offer, don't just regurgitate what's already available publicly. Focus on the portions that investors need to know, perhaps with some background for edification, and launch straight into what you believe it means for them and how your firm is prepared to respond. What makes intellectual capital strategic—for firm and investor alike—is the value-added perspectives the investment manager can provide on current events.

6. **Apply the stylistic principles of investment writing to your intellectual capital.**

   From visuals to storytelling, tone to vocabulary, intellectual capital is no different from other subgenres of investment writing in the way you choose to apply stylistic principles. For more, refer to Chapter 4.

The Elements of Intellectual Capital

Intellectual capital can capture any blend of the following:

- **Research:** Raw findings (such as data points and other information) that the firm has obtained firsthand or sourced from other parties
- **Analysis:** An examination and synthesis of findings and their subsequent interpretation
- **Insights:** An extra leap of interpretation—whether by connecting multiple ideas, extrapolating from available information, or relying on an intuitive understanding of something—that isn't necessarily obvious or evident, and that results in a penetrating vision or projection the firm can articulate to its clients
- **General knowledge:** Sundry facts and information imparted to the investor

Of the foregoing four, "insights" qualify as the most genuine form of "thought leadership"—the oft-used catchall term for forward-thinking perspectives and forefront ideas. Mark Truss, adjunct professor of insight discovery at Columbia University, reminds us that insights aren't facts or findings. They need to be *created*. And Scott Bedbury, former chief marketing officer of Nike and Starbucks, tells us how: Insights have far more in common with intuition and imagination than they do with deductive reasoning.

A portfolio manager once told me how he develops insights when evaluating countries in which to invest. Part of his assessment is straightforward: He reviews key economic and business indicators—gross-domestic-product growth, the unemployment rate, patterns of security issuance, the general health of the financial markets, the value of local currencies, imports and exports, and other indicators—to determine whether the macro environment is favorable for investing.

Then he digs deeper. He interviews government officials and parses their statements to glean hints of future economic policy. He looks at the intricate linkages between countries to examine their economic, social and geopolitical interplay.

Lastly, he looks for clues in more obscure places, such as the boards that govern central banks. Do they offer a seat at the table for representatives of a country's finance ministry? An affirmative answer would raise a red flag, because central banks are supposed to have the independence of regulating the money supply and making apolitical monetary-policy decisions without undue pressure from other branches of government. Such meddling would also lead this portfolio manager to wonder whether it's the symptom of a broader problem with a country's governance culture at large. Is its financial system strong enough to withstand shifts in the political climate and operate with integrity? Those are just some of his considerations for gauging political risk—the likelihood of investments suffering as a result of changes or instability in a country's leadership. Insightful thinking, indeed.

The marketplace is flooded with self-proclaimed insights, so if you wish to offer any through your intellectual capital, you had better have something to say that is both meaningful and defensible. Bob Buday, a thought-leadership advisor and co-founder of Bloom Group, proposes seven criteria for an insightful point of view:

1. **Novelty:** It should break new ground or at least advance a way of thinking about an issue.
2. **Focus:** It must have a single, overriding message that can be stated in one or two sentences.
3. **Relevance:** It ought to meet a specific market need or be of interest to the audience it targets.
4. **Validity:** It has to be supported by evidence.
5. **Practicality:** It needs to demonstrate that the solution it proposes can be implemented.
6. **Rigor:** It should have tight, consistent logic throughout.
7. **Clarity:** It must be communicated in language and concepts the target audience understands.

The Packaging of Intellectual Capital

Let's look at how intellectual capital can be rationalized and expressed editorially. Here again, much like when dealing with foundational literature, no single method is set in stone. Still, one can distinguish between four broad types of intellectual capital by the nature, purpose, and shelf life of their content:

1. Investment papers
2. Primers
3. Investment commentary
4. Surveys

One approach is to establish an individually branded series of publications for each type so as to differentiate them visually and editorially, make them recognizable to your readers, and lead them to know what to expect. Another is to produce a periodical journal—a sort of compendium—containing a collection of pieces on one or more topics.

Investment papers Investment papers—often called "whitepapers"—are descriptive ruminations about investment topics in long, expositional form. They typically contain some or all of the elements described earlier—research, analysis, insights, and general knowledge—while marshalling proof points to substantiate a claim, posit a thesis, or propose a concept. An investment paper may focus on any variation of the following agendas, or a combination of two or more of them:

1. **The case for investing in something**

   This category of paper presents an evergreen argument in favor of investing in a particular asset, or asset class. It may do so by focusing exclusively on the merits of the asset in question (i.e., "X is an attractive investment because it can provide benefits A, B, and C") or by framing the case as a solution to a problem ("The problem is Y, and the solution is to invest in X because of benefits A, B, and C").

   The problem/solution line of reasoning, when applicable, is especially compelling because it couches your argument in the context of an unwelcome situation that requires pressing resolution. It is also the option to which investors facing the problem you described could easily relate.

   For example, you can make the case for investing in offshore stocks by focusing on the opportunities they provide to gain returns, as well as on their diversification merits (such as low price correlation to domestic stocks). But you can also frame your case as a solution to the problem of a geographically homogenous portfolio, when asset values in a given region drop in unison and could result in significant losses, as they have during broad-based downturns throughout history.

   Alternatively, your paper can make the case for investing in something by virtue of comparison. For example, one portfolio manager authored a paper explaining how subprime mortgage-backed securities differ from subprime auto asset-backed securities in terms of the opportunities they offer.

   Investment papers of this kind enjoy longer shelf life than some of their topical counterparts, as explained next.

2. **A topical affair**

   Topical investment papers usually come in two flavors:

   a. The first type addresses an investment issue of immediate relevance, interest, or importance in relation to current events, market conditions, or a set of transient circumstances. For instance, one paper described a narrow window of opportunity to invest in deeply discounted bridge loans as a result of turmoil in the credit markets at the time. Another paper, which addressed a contemporaneous surge in commodity prices, attempted to explain that both speculative forces (i.e., opportunistic investors) and secular forces (i.e., natural growth in demand) were at play. It argued that commodities might exhibit price volatility in the short run but that, over the long haul, they remained a viable and attractive investment destination.

Topical papers of this type are timely and situationally driven, and thus have relatively limited shelf life.

b. The second type of topical paper is meant to explain general-interest subjects and describe the investment opportunity they represent. These subjects can span any area of commerce, research, or exploration—or any industry or trade you can imagine.

For example, suppose your firm offers a fund that invests in a variety of tech outfits, including companies that build highly sophisticated robots. You could develop a topical paper on the subject of robotics—the branch of science and engineering that deals with designing autonomous machines that can perform a range of tasks. Such a paper could explain to investors the domestic, commercial, and military uses of such machines, the technology behind their development, and the field's financial promise as an investment opportunity.

Topical papers of this nature tend to have long shelf life.

3. **A proposed investment approach or strategy**

Papers of this category suggest a particular way in which to invest— a strategy or plan of action for consideration—whether as an idea to achieve an investment objective or a technical way to address a pain point.

One firm, for example, published a paper outlining the process of making operational improvements in acquired companies to wring value from private-equity transactions. Another issued a paper on return-shaping strategies using derivatives in multi-asset portfolios.

The shelf life of such papers would depend on whether the approach or strategy they propose is tactical and perhaps opportunistic (i.e., short-term) or whether it is strategic (long-term).

4. **Investment research**

Papers of this category detail a scholarly study of an investment topic. They may include heavy quantitative analysis, provide insights, and offer practical conclusions. Some topic examples include:

- The effects of different taxation regimes on common models of asset allocation
- A behavioral analysis of different types of investment portfolios under market stress
- An examination of Active Share (a measure of how a portfolio's composition differs from that of its benchmark) and its relation to investment performance

The shelf life of papers like these depends on the usefulness and relevance of their research.

5. **A proposition and its intellectual rationale**

An investment paper can also be used to introduce any idea or make any argument while presenting the set of reasons or logical basis for it. One firm, for example, issued a paper explaining why investors should consider both rolling and trailing returns over long time frames to get a complete picture of an investment's risk/reward profile.

Storylines to Consider for Your Investment Paper As mentioned in the section titled "Piquing Investors' Interest" in Chapter 4, forging a compelling storyline will help draw readers to your paper and entice them to read it through. Each of the four types of papers we've just covered can interest investors—yet there could be other intriguing angles to your story, from the counterintuitive or paradoxical to the unexpected. You could also use your paper as an opportunity to debunk a myth, rectify a misconception, or refute a prevailing notion.

For example, let's say you're writing a paper on how investing in private real assets—namely farmland, timberland, and commercial real estate—can help diversify a portfolio by reducing its correlation with public markets. To whet investors' curiosity, you can lead into your story with a rhetorical, thought-provoking question, such as the following:

What do Brazilian forests, French vineyards, and San Francisco's business district—with all its skyscrapers—have in common?

You can see where this is headed.

Or imagine having to write a paper explaining how hedge funds are screened and evaluated for operational integrity by fund-of-funds managers—an arguably drab but crucial matter. With a bit of wordplay in your title, drama in your synopsis, and a nod to paradox and history in your opening paragraphs, you might be able to rouse some interest, as in the following hypothetical example:

DILIGENCE IS DUE, BUT SO IS IMAGINATION

To identify and manage operational risks from hedge funds, a typical checklist from last year's due diligence questionnaire is no longer enough. It's time to get creative.

Protecting against the unfortunate is a thankless task. You're in a constant chase to pinpoint the next elusive hazard and shield your subject from it. Your success is indicated by what doesn't happen (i.e., the result of prevention) rather than by what does. Uneventful times are good for you, yet they can lure you into dangerous complacency. And the slightest failure to achieve protection can overshadow your greatest prior accomplishments.

Enter operational risk management: Such is the task of protecting investors against losses that could result from exposure to hedge funds with inadequate or unscrupulous business practices. It's an exercise that requires continual refinement to detect the evolving risks of the marketplace.

Hedge funds offer a plethora of investment opportunities, to be sure, and the industry can certainly pride itself on a history of accomplishments since Alfred Winslow Jones pioneered the first-ever fund in 1949. Still, human fallibility is enough to keep operational risk managers hard at work on tomorrow's mission: to break the traditional molds of common due-diligence checklists and devise creative methods to extract more and better information on the operations of hedge funds.

Here we note some resourceful ways in which to approach the fund-screening process and detail a handful of key matters to consider in evaluating operational risks.

Primers   A primer is a piece that introduces an investment topic—typically as a prelude to a more in-depth discussion.

In some ways, primers are tricky to define, because they inhabit a fuzzy intersection of educational literature (explained later, in Part 3 of this chapter) and investment papers (explained previously). They're not quite the former, as the subjects they cover are more advanced than rudimentary and more specialized than general. On the other hand, they're not quite as dense as the latter.

Unlike investment papers, primers aren't meant to feature exhaustive research, analysis, or nuts-and-bolts information. To borrow the aviator's cliché, they serve the "30,000-foot view"—a high-level exploration of a topic for instructive purposes. As their name indicates, they exist to prime the investor on a subject as the baseline for deeper understanding and consideration. (Incidentally, you can also use primers to make the case for investing in an asset or pursuing a strategy, but try to keep it simple and reserve more detailed explanations for investment papers.)

There's no clear-cut rule for primer design. You can produce them to look and feel like brochures, with greater emphasis on color, imagery, and gloss. You can design them to appear like a full-fledged investment paper—perhaps with more text and graphs. Your choice would depend on the editorial direction you wish to pursue, content sophistication, and branding considerations.

To demonstrate the middle ground that primers occupy vis-à-vis educational literature and investment papers, let's look at how each of the three could cover the topic of, for example, distressed debt:

1. **The educational piece** would demystify the asset class for beginners by providing a definition (i.e., debt securities of companies experiencing financial hardship) and giving examples. It could then explain the rationale for investing in such securities (namely, the opportunity to buy debt at a deep discount and seek attractive returns by salvaging an operation and avoiding bankruptcy or default—perhaps through debt reduction or renegotiation). Finally, it could offer surface-level examples of the roles investors play in distressed-debt situations, as well as the benefits and risks involved.
2. **The primer** would delve into a deeper discussion of concepts in distressed-debt investing. It could show how distressed debt is manifest in credit spreads, prices, market trading, and market participants' expectations of future discounted cash flows. It could explain how the investment opportunities arise when the company is believed to have insufficient cash flow to service its debt—and when it may need in-court or out-of-court debt restructuring. Lastly, it could describe the bankruptcy process, the role of debtor-in-possession (DIP) facilities, and the importance of assessing security valuations to identify attractive opportunities.
3. **The investment paper** would discuss concrete strategies for investing in distressed debt based on the various degrees of investor involvement in the debt-restructuring process.

A primer can serve as powerful marketing literature—even if it isn't explicitly promotional. By exhibiting the intricacies, risks, and opportunities of a given subject, it subtly implies that your firm is also capable and well equipped to help the investor tackle it in practice.

Investment Commentary Investment commentary includes any piece of literature that expresses opinions, provides explanations, or offers prognoses concerning investment affairs.

It can focus on a sector, region, or type of security or asset. It can cover the markets at large. It can be a one-off, special-purpose piece—an ad hoc communication on the heels of an event or situation, such as a crisis, to explain the developments in question and their ramifications. Or, it can be offered in regularly scheduled periodicals—billed by some firms as a "market outlook" or "market playbook"—recapping the events that have taken place and their significance, as well as a point of view about the future. (The most common periodicals are weekly, monthly, quarterly, semiannual, and annual.)

Investment commentary can serve as a platform for stating viewpoints on any matter of interest to investors and their advisors. Years ago, one portfolio manager penned an opinion piece expressing how he believed a particular country—a major player on the global stage—could improve its economic policy, and suggested a roadmap for doing so. (He phrased his piece, cleverly, as an open letter to the country's policymakers.) Some portfolio managers publish travel diaries chronicling their firsthand impressions—social, economic, political, or otherwise—of destinations they visited and in which they invest or would consider investing.

Editorially speaking, there is more than one way to deliver commentary. One is to write a full-fledged paper detailing research, analysis, and perhaps insights. Another is to deliver it in the form of a presentation—a series of slides dominated by charts with accompanying bullet points. You can also produce a short blog highlighting your main points. (Non-written commentary can include podcasts and videos featuring investment professionals verbalizing their perspectives.)

Note that *investment* commentary isn't *fund-performance* commentary. The former, in keeping with other varieties of intellectual capital, is product-agnostic. The latter revolves around how a fund or strategy performed and why (more in Part 5 of this chapter on shareholder communications). Being product-agnostic doesn't mean you can't express investment views; it just means you need to be general about them. For example, you may write that you "favor Latin American bonds over stocks" in the coming quarter and explain the reasons for this view without citing any of your investment funds or strategies for investing in Latin America.

Consider this hypothetical executive summary of an annual commentary paper, whose forecasts are fictitious and meant purely for demonstration:

THE GREAT DIVERGENCE

How will economies, markets, and investment opportunities shape up in the year ahead?

Executive Summary

- The past year saw marked disparities in the growth patterns and economic policies of different regions.

- North America's and Asia's economies have accelerated, and their central banks are attempting to clamp down on inflationary pressures by hiking interest rates. We expect their equity markets to post attractive—if moderate—returns in the year ahead.

- In contrast, the central banks of Latin America and Europe are lowering rates given economic indicators that show signs of a potential slowdown in the offing. In these two regions, we favor bonds over stocks. Within their fixed-income sectors, we believe that rates (government bonds and interest-rate swaps) will outperform credit (corporate bonds).

Investor Surveys By surveying investors on their opinions, experiences, and attitudes—and publishing the results of your study—you can not only learn more about your clients, but also impart a valuable form of intellectual capital to the investor community.

Investors of all types find it instructive to learn about their peers, whether they are individual or institutional, mass retail or high-net-worth, young or elder. What challenges do they face? How do they view the current and future state of the markets through the prism of informed citizens and organizations? What does their average portfolio look like? What investment strategies are they pursuing, and what results have they experienced? Do they plan on altering their strategies? If so, how? Those are just some of many issues to examine toward understanding what's commonly billed as "the voice of the client."

Some firms conduct such surveys on a periodical basis—occasionally in partnership with providers of market intelligence and research, or with the financial media—and issue their findings, analyses, and insights in research reports. There are no rigid editorial guidelines for survey papers; you have plenty of creative leeway. Still, consider the following pointers:

1. Open with a message from your firm or one of its senior representatives, such as the CEO, chief marketing officer, or executive leading the client-facing functions in the organization. The letter can introduce the topic of the survey and its purpose, and provide some color on the audience that was surveyed. It can highlight the survey as an extension of the firm's commitment to understanding and serving its clients—and to advancing the investment profession as an industry player. Finally, it can express gratitude to the participants who agreed to be surveyed.
2. Follow with an executive summary highlighting key survey results and your interpretations of them.
3. Begin the report with an explanation of the methodology you constructed to administer the survey, including key features of your population sample and the techniques (numerical and qualitative) you employed to register responses.
4. Use charts and other visual exhibits to illustrate your findings.
5. Feature representative quotes from the survey's respondents as callouts throughout the report. The quotes can be anonymous, but try to select those reflecting the zeitgeist captured in your survey's results.
6. Conclude with a forward-looking thought about how investors should draw on the results for the future.

The Process of Writing Long-Form Literature

Unlike brief forms of investment literature, such as product profiles or short blog posts, lengthy pieces often require an organized, regimented process of development—from conception to final copy—especially if you're writing on behalf of an author other than yourself whom you may need to interview.

Let's make the likelier assumption that you are *not* the author. Either way, consider yourself fortunate—if for no other reason than the sense of fulfillment one could gain from long-form composition. Take it from author and sociologist Sara Lawrence-Lightfoot. Here's what she told journalist Bill Moyers in an interview years ago:

Each one of these books that I write is really a [...] new quest for me. I'm able to engage in new learning. And that's a huge, huge luxury. I think [writing is one of] those professions [that sustain] your curiosity throughout. You're able [and] very privileged to grow in it.[6]

Are you ready? Then you may need to perform any of the following steps—not necessarily all of them, and not necessarily in the following order—while potentially repeating some of them once or more:

1. Interviewing the author
2. Establishing a topic, editorial direction, and other parameters for the piece—including research, information sources, and proof points
3. Interviewing additional professionals throughout the organization as necessary to obtain information
4. Reviewing supporting materials (including transcriptions of interviews, presentations, videos, podcasts, and other recordings that may need to be transmuted into editorial form) and related literature from which to learn about the topic and obtain background information
5. Sketching a high-level outline
6. Formulating a more detailed outline—or perhaps a series of progressively deeper outlines toward fleshing out the piece (if you're outline is deep enough, you can "just add water" to arrive at your manuscript)
7. Drafting a fully formed manuscript for review
8. Working with the author on one or more rounds of revisions to solidify a final version

The steps you perform and their sequence will depend, among several factors, on the knowledge and materials you already have about the topic; on the author's preferences with respect to—and level of involvement in—the writing and editing process; and on your pace and time constraints.

When pressed to a critical deadline, align your work to three priorities: first accuracy, then speed, and finally style. Being correct is paramount. Being punctual in meeting deadlines is, of course, important in any business—yet secondary to accuracy. And while finesse and polish in your language are expected, they can only assume tertiary priority when stacked up against accuracy and speed.

To get a sense of how outlines can take shape, consider the following deep outline of a paper on why high-yield bonds in the United States could still make for an attractive investment in an environment of low interest rates and low yields:[7]

"THE CASE ENDURES FOR HIGH-YIELD BONDS"

Deep outline

- The concerns
  - Some investors are concerned that the attractiveness of high-yield bonds in the United States has fizzled.
  - Strong demand has bid up high-yield bond prices and limited the potential for future appreciation.
    [Exhibit 1 will feature a bar chart plotting high-yield bond prices over the past decade, up to the present, using a representative index.]
  - Demand has also reduced yields to new lows and tightened credit spreads to levels that no longer seem to adequately compensate investors for the risk of default.
    [Exhibit 2 will feature a line chart plotting the yields of high-yield bonds over the past decade, up to the present, using a representative index.]
  - Fanning investors' concern are U.S. interest rates, which have progressively declined to historic lows over the past 30 years. The prospect of higher rates may usher an inflection point for fixed income moving forward.
    [Exhibit 3 will feature a line chart plotting U.S. interest rates over the past 30 years, up to the present.]
- The questions
  - These issues raise a few key questions: Is there still a role for high-yield bonds in a diversified portfolio? If so, to what extent should investors reevaluate their current allocations to, or strategies for investing in, high-yield bonds?
- Answer #1: Diversification benefits
  - While demand for high-yield bonds and low interest rates may not persist at current levels, we do not believe they diminish the attractiveness of high-yield bonds as long-term portfolio diversifiers.
  - The past 30 years show their significant diversification benefits in relation to other asset classes:
    1. **Correlations:** They have exhibited low correlations to mortgage-backed securities and investment-grade corporate

bonds, relatively low correlations to equities, and negative correlations to U.S. Treasuries.

[Exhibit 4 will feature a correlation matrix using representative indexes for these assets.]

2. **Risk-adjusted returns:** They would have increased the risk-adjusted returns of a 100% U.S. Treasury portfolio.

[Exhibit 5 will plot an efficient frontier that includes a 100% U.S. Treasury portfolio, a 60% Treasury/40% high-yield portfolio, a 40% Treasury/60% high-yield portfolio, and a 100% high-yield portfolio—all using representative indexes.]

- **Answer #2: Relatively low sensitivity to interest-rate fluctuations**
  - High-yield bonds have been less sensitive to fluctuations in the interest rate when compared with other fixed-income assets.

  [Exhibit 6 will feature a comparison table showing the changes in the yields and total returns of high-yield bonds, Treasuries, investment-grade corporate bonds, and mortgage-backed securities—using representative indexes—for 10 different periods of interest-rate increases over the past 30 years.]

- **Answer #3: Attractive yields and lower default rates**
  - In relation to U.S. Treasuries, high-yield bonds still offer attractive yields.

  [Cite the latest spreads between U.S. Treasuries and a representative index of high-yield bonds.]

  - Although high-yield bonds carry a higher risk of default by definition, their default rate has declined.

  [Exhibit 7 will feature a line graph plotting the declining rate of high-yield bond defaults over the past decade.]

- **Answer #4: Focusing on credit quality and income**
  - We believe that moving forward, investors should use high-yield bonds not as a short-term tactical play for capital appreciation—but rather as a long-term, risk-managed strategy for income:
    1. **Credit quality:** We recommend that investors manage downside risks by focusing on higher quality segments of

(*Continued*)

the high-yield bond market to avoid exposure to potential defaults.

[Exhibit 8 will show the large disparity in the default rates between the riskiest and least risky segments of the high-yield bond market.]

2. **Income:** We expect income—not price appreciation—to drive the predominant share of total returns from high-yield bonds in the foreseeable future. Investors can benefit from using these bonds as long-term holdings to boost the income component of their portfolios.

- **Conclusion**
  - In spite of the current environment, we believe high-yield bonds remain valuable contributors to diversified portfolios for all the reasons mentioned.
  - All the same, we believe that investors in these bonds should emphasize long-term income while limiting their exposure to securities of higher credit quality.

PART 3: EDUCATIONAL LITERATURE

If investment in knowledge pays the best interest, as Benjamin Franklin once said, then investor literacy pays the best dividends.

Educated investors are good business. They're in a better position to understand your literature, gain a fuller appreciation of the products and services on offer, and make informed choices. No architecture of investment content is complete without educational material as one of its cornerstones, equipping investors with the elementary knowledge they need to establish familiarity with a topic.

Write your educational literature for a *tabula rasa* state of mind, with the assumption your readers are encountering the topic at hand for the very first time and require an anatomical explanation of its basics. Educational materials commonly take the form of introductory guides that serve to demystify a particular area of investment. Examples include literature with such titles as:

- A guide to derivatives
- An introduction to alternative investments
- Understanding convertible securities
- What are hedge funds?
- A fact sheet on master limited partnerships (MLPs)

You can also develop educational literature to explain the essentials of current events and their relevance to investors. For example, a change in the tax law or regulatory code of a country may justify issuing a fact sheet that explains the change and what it means for the investor.

The golden rule of explaining unfamiliar investment concepts is the very one dictionaries apply for their entries: Avoid the circular definition, which uses the term being defined as part of the definition itself, or assumes a prior understanding of that term. For example, consider the second of two alternative definitions to appear on a fact sheet about municipal bonds:

A circular definition:

A municipal bond is a bond issued by a city, county, state, or other government entity. It is used to fund capital improvements or refinance existing debt.

A non-circular, detailed and more elementary definition (preferred):

A municipal bond is a debt security issued by a government entity—such as a city or county—to borrow money for civic expenditures, including infrastructure development and community projects (e.g., the construction or refurbishment of bridges, sewer systems, roads, and schools). It is also used to refinance older loans at a lower rate of interest.

(Chapter 6 features additional techniques for explaining complex investment subjects.)

How you structure an educational piece depends on the anatomy of the topic. Here's one example—a suggested outline for "A Guide to Preferred Securities":

A GUIDE TO PREFERRED SECURITIES

Outline

[Slug: "Investments that combine stock and bond characteristics"]

- Introductory synopsis
  - Preferred securities combine features of both stocks and bonds. They may be suitable for investors who:
    1) Seek exposure to high credit quality at a low minimum investment; and

(Continued)

---

2) Are willing to accept reduced liquidity in exchange for relatively attractive yields in comparison with stocks or bonds.

- **An overview of preferred-security categories**
  1. Traditional preferred stock
  2. Trust preferred securities
  3. Enhanced trust preferred securities
  4. Senior notes
- **An overview of common investment features**
  - Low par values (minimum denominations)
  - High market accessibility
  - Predictable quarterly income
  - Payment deferral options
  - Call provisions and protection
  - Payment seniority and reduced risk of default

THREE QUICK FACTS ABOUT PREFERRED SECURITIES

1. In the event of bankruptcy, preferred securities rank ahead of common stock, but they are subordinated to debt.
2. Dividends on preferred stock are guaranteed and paid before dividends on common stock. However, dividends on preferred stock usually don't increase if the issuing company's profits rise.
3. Callable preferred securities enable the issuer to redeem the security before maturity.

- **Risk considerations**
  - Credit risk
  - Interest-rate risk
  - Call risk
  - Secondary-market risk

[Comparison table:] Preferred Securities at a Glance

- A comparison between each of the four categories of preferred securities by:
  - Maturity
  - Income type (dividend or interest)

- Eligibility for qualified dividend income
- Income payment deferral options
- Cumulative and non-cumulative dividends or interest
- Capital-structure seniority

PART 4: DIGITAL AND SOCIAL MEDIA

Investment literature requires a presence in online spheres if it is to gain reach and recognition in an era when print alone won't do. Popular avenues of digital- and social media publishing include:

- **Your firm's website,** which can house blogs, news items, videos, podcasts, interactive features that combine graphics and imagery with text, and other digital forms of content
- **Professional and social networking services,** such as LinkedIn and the Hearsay Systems platform for financial advisors, on which you can feature you firm's profile and publish posts
- **News and messaging services** such as Twitter
- **Video-sharing websites** such as YouTube
- **Podcast platforms** such as iTunes

(Your videos and podcasts can feature segments on investment issues, financial affairs, products, and strategies—whether scripted or narrated, and in the form of one-on-one interviews, expert panels, and roundtable discussions.)

When writing for digital and social media, follow many of the same editorial principles of content and style that apply to foundational literature, intellectual capital, educational materials, and other investor communications covered throughout this book. But remember that everything you pen will be displayed on screens—mostly small, as in handheld or portable devices—so be sure to create abridged adaptations of your writings to suit the online medium. Look at it as an exercise in "investment writing to go": It's to deliver snackable messages—in snappy, compact form—which are increasingly popular in an age of limited attention spans and digital canvases that aren't particularly flattering for content that requires more than a bit of scrolling.

To achieve high rankings in the search-engine results of readers' queries, write and tag your digital pieces with keywords most associated with your subject, and top them with headlines that appropriately reflect the body copy.

Your social media posts should be even briefer—crafted in virtually bite-sized pieces. In your writing, make a concerted effort to fixate readers' pupils and galvanize sharing. Social media is, after all, a sphere where content dissemination is democratized and mediated by its own participants.

Much of the so-called "viral content" out there—the kind that spreads infectiously online through extensive social sharing and links—tends to have shock value or be sensational or entertaining. Investment writing, however, should be more serious and substantive than light clickbait, so find creative ways to stimulate and provoke readers without diminishing gravitas, appearing flippant, or being offensive. (See the section titled "Piquing Investors' Interest" in Chapter 4 for some examples.)

Additionally, you could use tweets, social media posts, short website features, videos, and podcasts to promote long-form literature by giving readers the gist of the topic and then featuring a link. For example, suppose you published the investment paper on high-yield bonds whose outline example was featured in Part 2. You could announce its release on social media (while using hashtags and Twitter handles to associate your posts with relevant topics, people, organizations, and online discussions) in the following manner:

Tweet:
> *Reasons to maintain an allocation to #HighYieldBonds? Our CIO @SethSmarts has 5: [HYPERLINKED URL TO PAPER]*

LinkedIn post:
> [headline:]
> *The end for high-yield bonds? Not so fast*
> [synopsis:]
> *Despite rock-bottom yields, our CIO Seth Smarts believes that high-yield bonds continue to play a long-term role as portfolio diversifiers. Here's why: [HYPERLINKED URL TO PAPER]*

You could also compose an executive summary of the paper on one of your website pages and feature an option to download the full piece. Or how about a 500-word blog on the topic linking to the full paper? The options are manifold.

Then again, digital and social media posts don't necessarily require long-form counterparts. If the idea you wish to convey is sufficiently brief, write a self-contained post to express it, as in the following example:

Tweet:
> *We believe that uncertainty about quarterly earnings results next week is suppressing investors' appetite for #RiskAssets.*

In summary, digital and social media content can either shadow your other literature in condensed form, complement it, or do both. It allows you to interact with existing and prospective investors, advisors, and consultants through additional channels whose use has become both customary and expected. It enables your readers to access briefer, more targeted versions of your literature and consume it in multimedia form, assuming you also offer videos and podcasts. It makes use of platforms that enable quick publishing when market events and crises require rapid turnaround time. (Imagine a noteworthy development in the news that warranted a prompt reaction from your firm. Between writing, editing, design, and production, it might take longer to bring a full-on investment paper to market than it would to publish a short blog, website announcement, or social media post—or to record a five-minute video or audio segment featuring one of your portfolio managers.) Lastly, digital and social media content can help drive traffic to your firm's website and longer-form literature.

PART 5: SHAREHOLDER COMMUNICATIONS

The fifth and final category of investment content includes specific communications that target fund shareholders, such as:

- Official notices or frequently-asked-question (FAQ) sheets to the investor about such matters as shareholder-vote solicitations, product and organizational changes, capital gains, special occasions, and other matters of interest (refer to Chapters 3 and 4 for examples)
- Personal outreach from an investment or client-service professional in the form of a letter
- Newsletters featuring firm and product news, a roundup of recently published literature by your firm, and a calendar of upcoming events (similar to consultant newsletters highlighted in Chapter 3)
- Periodical reports (if applicable) about your firm's practices, achievements, and contributions in the realms of sustainable, socially responsible, environmentally minded, or impactful investing
- Fund-performance commentary

Publicly traded companies across industries—including those that are *not* investment outfits—issue communications to shareholders of their stock, such as annual reports and voting solicitations. But we'll limit this discussion to the communications that investment companies—both private and publicly traded—issue to the shareholders of their investment funds.

Let's take a closer look at fund-performance commentary—an obligatory element of the communication mix that warrants a closer look.

Fund-Performance Commentary

As mentioned in Chapter 1, investment firms deliver periodical communications to fund shareholders detailing performance information. In the United States, for example, registered investment companies need to produce semi-annual and annual reports on the performance of their mutual funds.

Performance commentary is a valuable opportunity for fund managers to weigh in with descriptive appraisals of their strategies. It's an occasion for them to demonstrate accountability, express their convictions and perhaps defend their positions, clarify where they stand with respect to market developments, and explain how they are preparing for the future. (As mentioned earlier in this chapter, fund managers can also issue special-purpose commentary in times of crisis or extraordinary events to assess the near- and long-term implications for their funds and discuss how they intend to address the developments at hand.)

There are multiple ways to structure fund-performance commentary. Here are the most basic suggested elements to include:

1. **Performance review and attribution**
   State the fund's performance for the period (specifically versus the benchmark, if applicable), and describe the key factors that affected its performance.
2. **Market review**
   Provide some background on the general state of the market and economic climate as it pertains to the fund's investment strategy.
3. **Contributors and detractors**
   List up to a handful of fund holdings that contributed most positively or negatively to the fund's performance, along with explanations. Alternatively or additionally, you can list sector, industry, or country contributors and detractors.
4. **Forward-looking perspective**
   Verbalize the portfolio managers' outlook for the fund and the markets in the coming period. Explain how they're prepared to address market developments and respond to them. Take the opportunity to reiterate their investment convictions if you see fit.
5. **Exhibits**
   Include tables and charts depicting the fund's performance, top holdings and related information.

Performance commentary is formal and applies many of the stylistic principles for official communications outlined in Chapter 4, including the need to refrain from colloquialisms—especially slang. Since commentary writing addresses fund performance and strategies, it is also technical. But keep it as accessible as possible for audiences of individual investors with basic knowledge. Break up long passages of text with meaningful subheads that reveal the narrative. Incorporate an executive summary or a shaded box with bulleted highlights. And don't skirt obliquely around the uncomfortable issues: Write in plain, straightforward language.

Consider select highlights from the fund performance commentary of an imaginary real estate securities fund:

INVESTORPRO EUROPEAN REAL ESTATE SECURITIES FUND

Performance for the Six Months Ended June 30, 2017

The InvestorPro European Real Estate Securities Fund posted a negative return of –7% for the period, compared with the –13% return of its benchmark.

There were two reasons for the fund's losses during this period:

1. **A general market downturn:** Investors grew concerned over slowing economic growth and political uncertainty in Europe, which induced them to retreat from stocks throughout the region. This retreat triggered an indiscriminate decline in stock values across the board, including those of real estate investment trusts (REITs).

2. **U.S. dollar appreciation:** The fund is unhedged, meaning that it does not hedge currency risk. Its advantage lies in offering increased diversification and allowing gains from overseas currency appreciation in addition to potential gains from the REITs in which it is invested. However, over the six-month period, the U.S. dollar rallied against the euro, causing the fund's European holdings to be worth less when converted back to dollars.

Notwithstanding, some of our stock choices cushioned the portfolio against the full effects of the downturn. The fund outperformed its benchmark by six full percentage points, thanks to overweight (i.e., larger-than-benchmark) positions in certain REITs that we believe have long-term appreciation potential.

(Continued)

Most Property Sectors Posted Losses

Of the fund's 10 property sectors, 8 declined during the 6-month period. The largest detractors to the fund's performance came from the regional mall and office sectors, which returned –9.2 percent and –8 percent, respectively.

Stock Choices Led to Some Downside Protection

These detractions were partly offset by stronger performance of other holdings, including an overweight position in Property Empire, an owner of residential properties for rent, which remained flat; and Dynamic Distributors, a proprietor of distribution facilities, which declined by just 0.1 percent.

We Maintain a Long View on European REITs

The fund's management team views the negative results for REITs over the period as an episodic downturn. As we see it, real estate continues to play an integral role in Europe's economy by:

- Offering housing to a growing population;
- Serving as a source of wealth and savings for individuals, families, and businesses; and
- Providing the infrastructure for commercial activity through office space, manufacturing and distribution facilities, and storage warehouses.

Despite the losses over this six-month period, we continue to believe in the long-term viability and growth opportunities among select real-estate stocks throughout Europe. We maintain sizable positions in these companies in anticipation of attractive returns in the years to come.

NOW THAT YOU'VE MAPPED ARCHITECTURE ...

... it's time to construct the edifice: an integrated body of investment content comprising your firm's foundational literature, intellectual capital, educational literature, content for digital and social media, and shareholder communications. Overlaying them is your content strategy—the choice of message, packaging, timing, channel, and audience—which should serve as a productive catalyst to investor relations.

Note that in recent years, firms have been paring down their use of print and are instead limiting their content offerings to the digital realm. Many firms offer downloadable content on their websites. Some even offer access to custom-tailored libraries of electronic content—through such devices as tablet computers and mobile phones—allowing easy navigation and portable consumption by investors, advisors and consultants.

NOTES

1. Israel Channel 2 News, March 14, 2017.
2. "Overview: A Newsletter for BlackRock Shareholders," BlackRock Distributors, Inc., September 2005.
3. Emile Hallez, "Invesco Reveals Worst Words to Use with Investors," Ignites, June 20, 2013.
4. Arianna Huffington, "It's Time to Retire Our Definition of Retirement," *The Huffington Post*, September 5, 2014. Available at www.huffingtonpost.com/arianna-huffington/its-time-to-retire-our-definition-of-retirement_b_5774878 .html and retrieved on August 19, 2017.
5. J.P. Morgan Asset Management, "Observations and Thoughts from the 2014 J.P. Morgan Retirement Symposium," *Converging Forces*, April 2014.
6. *Bill Moyers Journal*, PBS, May 8, 2009. Retrieved on September 17, 2017, from www.pbs.org/moyers/journal/05082009/transcript2.html.
7. This hypothetical outline is modeled on a paper by Kevin Lorenz, Jean Lin, and James Tsang from TIAA-CREF titled "The Enduring Case for High-Yield Bonds," April 2013.

How to Simplify Complex Investment Subjects

"This paper seems a great deal harder to read than it was to write."
—An imaginary investor critiquing an abstruse piece of
technical literature in discouragement

It's no exaggeration to assume that the slightest difficulty on the part of the investor in trying to understand what you wrote could be met with impatience or irritation, if not abandonment and a broken deal. Let that not intimidate but motivate you to be resourceful, find creative ways to untangle complex subjects, and make them easier to understand.

Are you up to the task? Then you must accept the unequal labor pact with your readers that goes along with it—and work hard so that they won't need to. You may break a mental sweat on occasion as your sort through intricate detail, trying to figure it all out, and synthesize it cohesively into accessible, elegant prose. But you'll reach immense satisfaction once you do.

Here are some common techniques for making dense material more graspable.

THINK BITS—NOT PIECES

Even the most intellectually voracious investors cannot be forced to bite off more than they can chew. So, feed them in bits rather than pieces: When confronted with an elaborate topic you need to explain, break it down to smaller components, and consider the use of labeled bullets to explain each component. For an example of how to do this, refer to the section on investment-process articulation in Part 1 of Chapter 5. For another, refer to the section on how to break down lengthy RFP responses, also in Part 1 of Chapter 5.

Here's one more example. Imagine having to explain to investors that the portfolio manager of their global government-bond fund is undertaking a "curve-steepener" trade. The mere encounter with such a topic is enough to unsettle quite a few readers and encourage them to ditch your writing in favor of a stiff drink—or perhaps a night out on the town. But by delivering it in step-by-step nuggets, you can make the topic more digestible. Let's start with some background in case you are unfamiliar with this kind of trade.

A curve steepener is a strategy that aims to benefit from widening differences between yields of shorter-maturity bonds (for example, a five-year government bond) and those of longer-maturity bonds (such as a 30-year bond). For the difference to widen, yields of the former would need to decrease and those of the latter to increase. These two simultaneous trends would cause the so-called "yield curve"—which plots bond yields of different maturities along a timeline—to steepen, as illustrated in Figure 6.1.

(As an aside, under normal market conditions, longer-maturity yields are typically higher to compensate investors for the risks associated with the time it takes for a bond's principal to be fully repaid.)

The yield of a bond is the interest it pays, divided by its price. For the yield to rise, the bond's price would need to fall, and for the yield to decline, its price would need to increase. Hence, a trade that stands to profit from a steepening yield curve involves long positions in shorter-maturity bonds

FIGURE 6.1   A yield curve

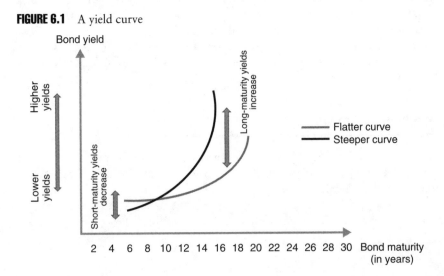

to gain from price increases—and short positions in long-maturity bonds to benefit from price declines.

If all this sounds dense to you, you're not alone. But at least you could help the investor by dividing the idea into two parts, as follows in this hypothetical example:

> *In the United Kingdom, InvestorPro's Global Government Bond Fund has entered into a so-called "curve-steepener" trade—one that could benefit from a steepening yield curve—consisting of two positions:*
>
> 1. *A long position in 5-year gilts (pound-denominated British bonds) to gain from potential price increases that would result in falling yields; and*
> 2. *A short position in 10-year gilts to profit from possible price decreases that would result in rising yields.*

By the way, you could also include the illustration just shown to depict the concept, which brings us to the next technique.

VISUALIZE THE IDEA FOR YOUR READERS

As mentioned in Chapter 4, charts, diagrams, and illustrations are useful for conveying complex information in pictorial form. The section on how to formulate a case study in Part 1 of Chapter 5, for example, featured a diagram depicting the multilateral relationships between an insurance company's general account, the returns on its investments, and the company's annuity policyholders.

You can also use infographics. Elegantly defined by author Bernard Marr, an infographic is an artistic representation of data and information using different elements such as graphs, pictures, diagrams, narratives, timelines, and checklists. An infographic can take the form of a one- or multiple-page storyboard containing a sequence of illustrations with titles and written text underneath—such as captions or bulleted lists—to explain an idea. It can also be a single image.

Figure 6.2 shows one clever example of how to explain a company's capital structure, which is the distribution of the types of debt and equity that make up its finances. The infographic uses the cabin configuration and travel classes of an airplane as a metaphor for the seniority of different segments of capital. (The many who fly coach and must endure the cramped quarters of narrow seating will commiserate with their subordinate siblings in common stock, who also lack preferential treatment.)

FIGURE 6.2   A company's capital structure is like aircraft seating

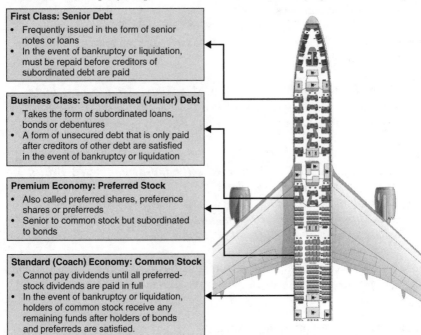

First Class: Senior Debt
- Frequently issued in the form of senior notes or loans
- In the event of bankruptcy or liquidation, must be repaid before creditors of subordinated debt are paid

Business Class: Subordinated (Junior) Debt
- Takes the form of subordinated loans, bonds or debentures
- A form of unsecured debt that is only paid after creditors of other debt are satisfied in the event of bankruptcy or liquidation

Premium Economy: Preferred Stock
- Also called preferred shares, preference shares or preferreds
- Senior to common stock but subordinated to bonds

Standard (Coach) Economy: Common Stock
- Cannot pay dividends until all preferred-stock dividends are paid in full
- In the event of bankruptcy or liquidation, holders of common stock receive any remaining funds after holders of bonds and preferreds are satisfied.

For more on bringing your information and data to life through artwork, there are specialized books to consult, including the recommended following:

> *The Wall Street Journal Guide to Information Graphics: The DOs and DON'Ts of Presenting Data, Facts and Figures*, by Dona M. Wong (W. W. Norton & Company, 2010)
>
> *The Visual Display of Quantitative Information*, by Edward R. Tufte (Graphics Pr, 2001)

START WITH A PREAMBLE

When writing about a complex subject matter, imagine yourself delivering an explanation to an investor seated before you. Having shook her hand—and after exchanging some pleasantries, perhaps about the weather—you would likely begin with some prefatory words as a warmup, no?

Very well: Apply the same principle in writing, and preface the heart of the matter with an explanatory preamble. In this example, you will need to describe a fund of your firm's that features a long/short strategy with an asymmetrical risk/reward profile. Here's how you might start:

> *All investment strategies share a common aim: to tilt the odds of a gain in the investor's favor. We take this aim one step further in also attempting to limit the downside when things go wrong, or create what we call an asymmetry between the risks and the potential rewards.*

Aha! Bracing herself, your investor now has a general idea of what's coming. You could then proceed:

> *How do we achieve this asymmetrical risk/reward profile? By identifying opportunities to capitalize on a company's business situation and then taking two simultaneous positions—long and short—in two securities, each tied to a different part of the company. In so doing, we aim to profit from Favorable Event X while concurrently limiting any potential downside from Unfavorable Event Y.*

At this point you're ready to get into specifics:

> *For example, suppose Company A is suffering from weak and deteriorating fundamentals. We would buy a credit default swap on that company—the equivalent of a short position—to profit in the event of a credit default.*
>
> *Yet there's a cost to holding that swap, known as the cost of carry. To defray that cost, we would purchase a basket of senior debt securities of the company, and then use the interest on those securities to pay for the swap. These securities enjoy seniority over bonds in the event Company A goes bankrupt or is liquidated. On account of their seniority, our strategy could benefit from limited downside during the intervening time waiting for the possibility of profiting from the credit default swap.*
>
> *In this fashion, we seek to create an asymmetry that favors upside potential—the possibility of gaining from our short position through the credit default swap—while aiming to reduce the risk of incurring a high expense or a loss in the process.*

LAY OUT A TABLE

Tables are an effective way to display multipart information for juxta-positional or comparative purposes. For example, consider Table 6.1, in which Ira Jersey, chief U.S. interest-rate strategist at Bloomberg, compares three types of currency-management strategies for U.S. investors across five parameters.

USE A FRAME OF REFERENCE, ANALOGY, OR METAPHOR

Some numbers are just too big to fathom, so it helps to put them in perspective. In 2006, the transaction-services division of a large corporate and investment bank described itself as processing $3 trillion in funds each day, a number so gargantuan as to be rendered meaningless—unless one realizes that $3 trillion had been more than the entire annual gross domestic product of France the year earlier. Such analogies can give investors a better sense of proportion.

Metaphors can also make complex ideas comprehensible. Martin Leibowitz and Anthony Bova, two investment researchers at Morgan Stanley, introduced an original way to explain the differences between three types of investment returns and the strategies used to achieve them:

1. **Market returns (or beta)**, which can be obtained passively through low-cost index funds that "feed off the return premiums that are broadly available to all"
2. **Incremental returns in excess of the market (or implicit alpha)** that can be obtained semi-passively (i.e., without major effort or taking on significantly more risk)
3. **Attractive returns in excess of the markets (or alpha)** that are derived from sheer manager skill and require a wholly active effort

To animate the distinctions between (2) and (3), which are subtle but important, they borrowed metaphors from the primordial occupation of food fetching—and deployed them masterfully in the following passage of their award-winning article, *Gathering Implicit Alphas in a Beta World*:[1]

> *In a sense, taking advantage of the implicit alphas that are truly available—and digestible—lies somewhere between passive beta-grazing and aggressive hunting for active alphas. To push the metaphor one step further, implicit alphas can enrich the diet of herbivores who are willing to raise their sights to include a limited amount of low-hanging fruit and berries (and maybe even nuts).*

TABLE 6.1 Overview of Currency-Management Strategies for U.S. Investors

Currency-Management Strategy	How is the strategy enacted?	Rationale	Restrictions for Free-Floating Currencies	Restrictions for Managed Currencies	Caveats
Periodic diversification	By holding a basket of securities in a variety of currencies while periodically trimming or increasing exposures to individual currencies on the basis of expected currency movements	Providing a cushion against the volatility of individual currencies	None	None	Vulnerable to long-term uptrends and downtrends in the U.S. dollar
Hedging	By holding securities denominated in non-U.S. currencies and then hedging them back to the dollar in the spot market, or through currency forwards or swaps	Curbing the risk that a currency could weaken against the dollar	None	Can only be done in the non-deliverable forward (NDF) market	Costs money, and its success hinges on good timing
Short-selling	By augmenting a portfolio with independent short positions in select currencies	A more assertive way to express a negative outlook on a currency	None	Difficult or impossible because of government and liquidity restrictions	Costs money and is susceptible to losses if the currency appreciates, but can be performed independently of other investments

Going even further into the metaphoric wilderness, it perhaps should be noted that some berries could be poisonous. Finally, while omnivores are fairly rare in nature, they may be the most popular species in the financial markets.

Implicit alphas are thus quite distinct from active alphas. Both forms of alpha offer the potential for enhanced return, and they can sometimes be combined to create exceptional opportunities. All the same, they are quite different concepts, and are pursued in different ways.

- *Active alphas must be hunted.*
- *Implicit alphas can be gathered.*

GIVE AN EXAMPLE

Describing a single occurrence of a concept in action—including plain arithmetic, if applicable—is a surefire way to make an abstraction concrete and enable investors to form a picture of that concept in their minds.

Let's say you wish to describe how a put option works. You could go about it in the following manner:

- Suppose you believe that the purchase price of stock X will go down in value—beneath $10 a share—sometime within the next 4 weeks.
- You could buy a put option from Mr. Choice that gives you the right to sell 10 shares of stock X to him at a price of, say, $10 a share any time between now and then.
- If the shares fall to $5 and you exercise that option, you can purchase 10 shares of stock X for $5 in the market and sell the shares to Mr. Choice for $10.
- Your profit would be $50 (calculated by multiplying the price difference of $5 by 10 shares) minus the premium you would have to pay to buy the put option.

* * *

These six techniques, which can be used individually or in combination, are just some of the popular ways to simplify complex topics for your investors.

NOTE

1. Published in the Spring 2007 issue of *The Journal of Portfolio Management* (Vol. 31, No. 1), and winner of the 9th annual Bernstein Fabozzi/Jacobs Levy Award for Best Article.

CHAPTER 7

How to Make Investment Writing Legally Compliant

You might not have chosen the legal profession in becoming an investment writer. But the legal profession, in many ways, has already enlisted you—and will be paying you frequent visits over the course of your occupation. Keep the figurative counsel's cap at your desk and be prepared to don it as you write, because you'll need to conform to a host of rules and restrictions about *what* you can say to investors and *how* you can say it.

In many jurisdictions throughout the world, the investment business is highly regulated, and firms are bound by a fiduciary responsibility—one involving a legal and ethical relationship of trust with investors—to place a client's interests ahead of their own. That responsibility extends to you, as the communicator and mouthpiece of your firm, in the way you sort and express your thoughts; couch, present, and illustrate ideas; and choose your words. It's a deliberative process that requires circumspection at every step.

Failing to comply with regulatory requirements could result in misleading information to the investor and risks harming your firm—whether by damaging its reputation, subjecting it to such penalties as fines or sanctions, or heightening the potential for future litigation.

Rest assured that you'll have guardians to help you out—the specialists of your firm's legal and compliance department. Think of them as reverse gatekeepers: Not a word leaves the firm or sees the light of day without their review and approval to ensure your writing meets regulatory standards. Still, you'll need at least a general ability to distinguish compliant from noncompliant writing at the onset—and learn to recognize key pitfalls—so that by the time a legal specialist reviews your work, it will have already met a host of essential criteria.

Your initial legal qualification will help streamline and expedite the review process. It will allow the reviewer to focus on recondite issues and restrictions you might not have anticipated. It will also enable you to wrest editorial control over your message: The more legally airtight and unassailable your writing, the less you'll need to negotiate content during the review stage, and the faster you can launch your paper boat onto the tide, so to speak.

Rules and regulations for the legal compliance of investment writing vary by firm and jurisdiction. Some regional authorities of the world's largest financial markets include the U.S. Securities and Exchange Commission (SEC) and Financial Industry Regulatory Authority (FINRA); China's Securities and Banking Regulatory Commissions (CSRC and CBRC); Japan's Financial Services Agency; the Bank of England's Financial Conduct and Prudential Regulation Authorities; Brazil's *Comissão de Valores Mobiliários*; the Securities and Exchange Board of India (SEBI); Canada's Office of the Superintendent of Financial Institutions (OSFI); and Germany's BaFin (or *Bundesanstalt für Finanzdienstleistungsaufsicht*—quite a mouthful for non-German speakers). Many investment firms across the globe also have their own internal legal guidelines to maintain or exceed the standards expected of them externally.

Regardless of your jurisdiction, there are fundamental legal and ethical principles that apply to the external communications of an investment firm. Whether they target the general public, current or prospective clients, financial advisors, consultants, or other intermediaries—and whether they are delivered electronically or in print—these communications include:

- Shareholder communications, such as performance commentary, personal letters, official notices, and account statements
- Invitations to calls, webcasts, and conferences
- Press releases, newsletters, and other circulars
- Promotional content and sales materials, such as foundational literature (e.g., brochures, product profiles, pitch books, and case studies), advertisements, presentations and telemarketing scripts
- Research and informational literature, from intellectual capital to educational materials
- Digital content such as videos, podcasts, website copy, and e-mail
- Social-media postings
- Reprinted materials from other sources such as trade publications or newspaper articles

Broadly speaking, investment writing should be fair and balanced. It should deliver a clear and evenhanded message that constitutes an adequate representation of your idea or offering, in good faith and honest dealing. It should provide a sound basis for the investor on which to evaluate your proposition. It ought not to contain misstatements, distortions, exaggerations, or unwarranted claims—nor should it make material omissions or seek to mislead readers in any way, such as when presenting selective information (also known as cherry-picking) without qualifying it or disclosing its limitations. It must include all the material facts, disclose all risks and caveats, and never conceal or understate the perils or potential disadvantages of what you put forward for consideration. Finally, back up your factual assertions with proof and, if applicable, cite your sources.

How are these principles practiced in everyday writing? Let's review a host of guidelines in connection with some of the most common situations you'll encounter.

AVOID ABSOLUTES, SUPERLATIVES, AND DEFINITIVE STATEMENTS...

... unless you can fully substantiate them with evidence or attribute them to a reputable source—or unless they are demonstrably unimpeachable.

Remember this guideline whenever you feel your enthusiasm getting the best of you, your fingers straying a bit too far afield to key in such words as *best, largest, first, last, highest, strongest, most, fullest, optimal, complete, supreme, perfect, lowest, weakest, least, cheapest, fastest, all, nothing, barring none,* and their likes.

Yes, it's a common impulse of persuasion—albeit one that is to be resisted, or at least tamed. Is the fund you offer truly the largest by assets under management in its category, or the highest performer? Cite an official ranking. Was your organization indeed the first to have introduced a product or strategy? Show the historical record and mention dates.

If you must use superlatives, qualify them as subjective assessments or value judgments—and be sure to couch your objectives or ideals (e.g., attractive returns, satisfied investment goals, minimum risks) as *pursuits, endeavors, aspirations,* or *possibilities* rather than a *fait accompli.* For example:

Not Compliant:	Compliant:
At InvestorPro, our portfolio managers work on generating high returns by gaining exposure to the most attractive assets.	At InvestorPro, our portfolio managers **aim** for high returns by **seeking** exposure to **what they believe** are the most attractive assets.
InvestorPro's team of portfolio managers establishes the most appropriate series of metrics for analyzing companies in which to invest.	InvestorPro's team of portfolio managers establishes **what it deems** the most appropriate series of metrics for analyzing companies in which to invest.
We alter our mix of holdings as often as necessary, **thereby minimizing** risks.	We alter our mix of holdings as often as necessary **in an effort to minimize** risks.

Not Compliant:	Compliant:
Political uncertainty in the regions where we invest may have an effect on returns in the coming months.	Political uncertainty in the regions where we invest may have an effect on **prospective** returns in the coming months.
Our ability to take long and short positions—without constraints—allows us to generate simultaneous returns from price appreciation and depreciation.	Our ability to take long and short positions—without constraints—**grants us the potential** to generate simultaneous returns from price appreciation and depreciation.

Avoid making unwarranted claims and assurances about prospects, such as a supposed ability to provide safety, calm, stability, security, peace of mind, or satisfaction.

Unless they are self-evident, factual assertions require specifying a source and date of attribution—whether in the body copy or a footnote. Here are some examples:

- Yields on 10-year Turkish bonds (lira notes) have jumped 70 basis points over the past four days.
- There is an increase in the number of private-equity deals underpinned by accommodative loan covenants, with more relaxed assurance requirements and lighter amortization schedules.
- Consumer confidence in Mexico continues to improve and is above the long-run average.
- Institutional investors in Asia are becoming more averse to risks.

Specifically, in the last three examples, you may also need to cite quantitative or descriptive (soft) indicators revealing the phenomenon you're describing. For example, what is your gauge for estimating the volume of accommodative private-equity deals? What indicator are you using to describe consumer confidence in Mexico? How is greater risk aversion expressed by Asian investors?

There are also restrictions on claiming that something is incontrovertible or giving the impression, by way of preface, that your statement is not open to dispute. Take the following two examples:

Example #1:	Example #2:
The truth is, markets go up and down.	The fact is, it makes more sense to invest in X than in Y to achieve greater capital appreciation.

The first statement would handily pass muster with your legal department: It is too obvious to be doubted. As an aside, it's not only a *truth* but also a *truism* (read: hackneyed).

The second statement might be too definitive in certain contexts and could get you in trouble if, for whatever reason, X no longer remains the "more sensible" investment; if it falls short of delivering greater capital appreciation; or if it fails to achieve capital appreciation at all. Consider a more reserved alternative that still provides something instructive for the investor to consider—only without staking out such an indubitable claim for itself:

Not Compliant:	Compliant:
The fact is, it makes more sense to invest in X than in Y to achieve greater capital appreciation.	**Amid present market conditions,** it **may** be more sensible to invest in X than in Y in order to enjoy greater capital appreciation.

Consider additional examples of definitive statements—ones that may be true but cannot be fully substantiated, are difficult to substantiate, or are rooted in value judgments—and ways to qualify them:

Not Compliant:	Compliant:
During the recent downturn in the markets, **virtually every investor/most investors** suffered.	During the recent downturn in the markets, **many investors** suffered.
We are witnessing **unprecedented** demand for consumables.	We are witnessing **perhaps one of the highest levels** of demand for consumables **in recent memory.**
The difficulties in the market seem manageable.	The difficulties in the market seem manageable **from our point of view.**
There are no convincing explanations for the precipitous spike in credit spreads.	**To the best of our knowledge,** there are no convincing explanations for the precipitous spike in credit spreads.

YOU CAN BE PREDICTIVE—BUT NOT PROMISSORY

It was during the heyday of peace negotiations in the Middle East—back in the mid-1990s—when the late Yitzhak Rabin was asked how confident he felt that peace would someday prevail in region. Rabin replied, "It's not advisable to become a prophet."[1] This nugget of history, aside from its tragic irony, contains sage advice for the investment writer.

Investing is, by definition, an anticipatory activity aimed at capitalizing on a perceived future, and it is predicated on forecasts. Take away the ability of investment professionals to issue their prognostications, and you might as well sentence them—and all us writers—to eternal silence.

Yet there's a fine line between a prediction and a prophecy. The latter isn't just inadvisable but prohibited. The former is legitimate—so long as you qualify it as a possibility rather than a certainty. Thus:

Not Compliant:	Compliant:
The demand for alternative fuels **will** rise and benefit biodiesel producers.	The demand for alternative fuels **may** rise and benefit biodiesel producers.

A more cautious legal reviewer may require an additional qualifier stressing that even if demand for alternative fuels rises, it may not necessarily benefit biodiesel producers in particular:

*The demand for alternative fuels **may** rise and **potentially** benefit biodiesel producers.*

You may also qualify a prediction as an opinion, like so:

***Our portfolio managers believe** the demand for alternative fuels **will** rise and benefit biodiesel producers.*

If you'd like to present your prediction as a likely occurrence, qualify it as a subjective judgment or cite a reputable source. Hence:

Not Compliant:	Compliant:
There's a good chance the secondary market for private debt will recover.	**In our estimation,** there's a good chance the secondary market for private debt will recover.
	There's a Y% chance the secondary market for private debt will recover, **according to study X as of [DATE].**

Even when predicting an occurrence that is widely anticipated by sheer logic, avoid definitive statements for anything you cannot absolutely guarantee. Instead, use softer substitutes that imply *expectation* rather than *presumption*, like so:

Not Compliant:	Compliant:
As technology enables information to flow more rapidly, the capital markets **will** become more efficient.	As technology enables information to flow more rapidly, the capital markets **should** become more efficient.

Look for ways to sidestep promissory statements—such as by playing with metaphors, phrasing your proposition in the form of a question, recasting it as a viewpoint, or negotiating verbal minefields in other creative ways—as in the following hypothetical examples of investment-paper titles:

Not Compliant:	Compliant:
The Bull Market Isn't Going Anywhere	The Persistent Bull: Why We Think Markets Will Continue to Climb Next Year
E-commerce Companies: Ripe For Investment *(a promissory statement of timing)*	The Stores of E-Commerce Are Open for Investment
Spain: The Next Comeback Story for Investors *(a value judgment that may not be grounded in fact or apply to all investors)*	Spain: The Next Comeback Story for Investors?
Trading patterns reflect pure optimism *(a presumptuous value judgment that may not reflect actual sentiment)*	Trading patterns reflect "pure optimism" *(you can use an attributable quotation)*

BE SPECIFIC ENOUGH FOR CLARITY—YET GENERAL ENOUGH TO ACCOMMODATE EXCEPTIONS

The investment world embodies two opposing spheres. The first is one of precision: It involves performance metrics and measurement, pricing, numerical analyses, accounting, transaction mechanics, and processes. The second contains the vagueness, randomness, and unpredictability that govern social sciences, as expressed in the capricious forces of supply and demand. These two spheres make investments a tricky subject to write about: You must be definite in some respects while also allowing room for the anomalous, unknown, or unforeseen.

For example, a basic principle of bond investing is that interest rates and bond prices generally move in opposite directions—with an emphasis on *generally*. It makes sense that when rates rise, existing bonds that pay a fixed coupon would gradually decrease in value. But who is to say that this should always be the case? Theoretically, if investors found reason to cling to their bonds no matter what, bond prices would turn impervious to rate fluctuations.

Similar caveats apply to any so-called "law" of the markets: Adding small but significant words of reservation—such as *generally, typically, commonly, usually, mostly, broadly, normally, widely, ordinarily, traditionally*—are we missing any?—can spell the difference between legal compliance and legal liability. Consider these examples:

Not Compliant:	Compliant:
An uptick in interest rates **would** cause bond yields to rise.	An uptick in interest rates **could/should** cause bond yields to rise.
Our fund invests in residential properties, with the understanding that greater demand for housing **will** raise the price of real estate.	Our fund invests in residential properties, with the understanding that greater demand for housing **tends to/is expected to/may** raise the price of real estate. *(Greater demand for housing may not necessarily raise the price in the event of more construction and greater supply.)*

Not Compliant:	Compliant:
Investors have shifted away from small-cap stocks into less risky assets, such as ultra-short municipal bonds.	Investors have shifted away from small-cap stocks into **traditionally** less risky assets, such as ultra-short municipal bonds. *(No one can guarantee that a municipality would not default.)*

Even the most seemingly obvious rules of investing may not always produce the intended result. Diversification, for instance, has failed to shield investors from losses during certain periods of severe market stress throughout history. In quant terms, they are known as periods when "all correlations go to one," or when the prices of most or all asset classes across the board move down in unison. Hence:

Not Compliant:	Compliant:
There's an obvious benefit to owning a diverse basket of securities, which **serves** as a stabilizing factor throughout the market's gyrations.	**We see a benefit** to owning a diverse basket of securities, which **can serve** as a stabilizing factor throughout the market's gyrations.

TIME-STAMP ANYTHING THAT'S IMPERMANENT

As circumstances change, so will your liability for anything you say that will not hold true forever:

Not Compliant:	Compliant:
Inflation is at an all-time high.	Inflation is **currently** at an all-time high.
	As of [DATE], inflation is at an all-time high.

CHERRIES ARE NOT FOR PICKING—AND SECURITIES COME AT A PRICE

To avoid the possibility of misleading the investor, you cannot selectively present information that bolsters your case, favors your agenda, or benefits your cause without disclosing other material information that does not.

For example, suppose you wrote a favorable investment review of a country and, to make your case, anecdotally singled out the names of a few local companies that do very well. Such mentions could be considered an inadequate demonstration of your thesis—what about other companies that may be floundering or failing?—and thus a prohibited instance of cherry-picking.

On the other hand, you may be able to cite individual securities as representative examples of a broader idea in a fairer context. Let's say you're writing a brochure on the prospects of supercomputing and wish to mention some of the world's major manufacturers in your piece by way of example. Your legal reviewer may approve, provided that you disclose whether your company invests in them and to what extent (e.g., "The InvestorPro Technology Fund had 35% invested in **Supercomputer Manufacturer A** and 25% in **Supercomputer Manufacturer B**, as of [DATE]").

NEGOTIATE GRAY AREAS WITH YOUR LEGAL REVIEWER

When it comes to communication—as with any soft skill—there are plenty of murky zones that don't readily conform to a category or lend themselves to unequivocal judgment. Try to work them out through give-and-take with your legal reviewer, assuming you have a receptive partner for negotiation.

References to *opportunities*, *possibilities*, and *chances*, to name just a few, are common focal points of deliberation. On one side are those who claim that *opportunity* requires no further qualification because it is just *that*: a set of circumstances making it possible to do something. They have a point. After all, there is no guarantee that an opportunity proper—with or without action—would result in a positive or negative outcome.

Some legal reviewers occasionally disagree. In certain contexts, they claim that references to *opportunity* could create a promissory impression, imply a guarantee, or induce a course of action without the requisite reservations. They, too, have a point. Consider the justifiable verdicts they might render for the following:

Not Compliant:	Compliant:
Present circumstances are creating a buy opportunity for asset X.	Present circumstances **may be** creating a buy opportunity for asset X.
(This statement implies a promise that it's safe to buy even though it references an opportunity rather than an outcome.)	**We think** present circumstances are creating a buy opportunity for asset X.

Not Compliant:	Compliant:
The market for exchange-traded funds is exponentially larger today and **thus** benefits investors with more opportunities. *(Even though there is no assurance of an outcome, this is a promissory declaration of benefit.)*	The market for exchange-traded funds is exponentially larger today and **may therefore** benefit investors with more opportunities.
The risks of investing in solar-panel producers do not negate the opportunity for returns, given the popular rise in demand for clean energy. *(This judgment of risk and reward needs to be qualified or substantiated.)*	The risks of investing in solar-panel producers, **as we see them**, do not negate the opportunity for returns, given the popular rise in demand for clean energy.

Then again, some realms are hazier:

Borderline Compliant:	Safely Compliant:
Opportunities abound to invest overseas.	Opportunities to invest overseas merit exploration.
The government of country X is enacting measures to boost the economy and creating investment opportunities.	The government of country X is enacting measures to boost the economy, **possibly** creating investment opportunities.
InvestorPro launched an exchange-traded fund designed to outperform the market in a rising-rate environment. *(The fund's design doesn't necessarily ensure that it will indeed outperform, but a conservative legal reviewer might choose safer phrasing.)*	InvestorPro launched an exchange-traded fund that is designed **with the objective of** outperforming the market in a rising-rate environment.

USE CAUTION WHEN NAVIGATING WORD SUBTLETIES

To avoid misleading the investor (and also reduce your chances of being edited by a legal reviewer), be judicious about every word choice and what it connotes in the context at hand. It helps to distinguish between *soft* and *strong* words, such as the following:

In the "Soft" Column:	In the "Strong" Column:
X **may** happen.	X **is likely** to happen/X **can** happen.
We **think** that...	We're **confident** that...
We **maintain**...	We **assert**...
Investors **may** consider...	Investors **should** consider... / Investors **ought to** consider
Potential	Prospective

Here are some examples of admissible soft language and its strong, inadmissible counterpart:

Not Compliant (Too Strong):	Compliant:
Geographic boundaries **should not** determine your strategy as a global investor.	Geographic boundaries **don't need to** determine your strategy as a global investor.
Diplomatic relations between Country A and Country B have been restored—and investors **have every reason** to be optimistic.	Diplomatic relations between Country A and Country B have been restored—and investors **may have good reason** to be optimistic.
The investment landscape in Scandinavia **is more promising than ever.**	The investment landscape in Scandinavia **appears to hold more promise.**

AVOID REDUNDANT QUALIFICATIONS

Protecting your firm—and doing everything you can to avoid misinforming the investor—are imperatives. But even verbal hedging has its upper limit of prudence beyond which you risk being perceived as lacking all conviction. Here are three examples:

Prudent:	Highly Cautious:	Excessive:
In our view, technology suppliers for motor vehicles stand to benefit from dramatic growth in the years ahead.	**In our view,** technology suppliers for motor vehicles **may** stand to benefit from dramatic growth in the years ahead.	**In our view, there's a possibility** that technology suppliers for motor vehicles **may** stand to benefit from **potentially** dramatic growth in the years ahead.

UNLESS YOU'RE PERMITTED, DO NOT DISPENSE INVESTMENT ADVICE

Some firms may not—or do not wish to—provide advice in a fiduciary capacity, whether because of their mandate in a particular jurisdiction or their internal legal guidelines. Often they will disclose such a limitation as variations of the following:

Firm X is not undertaking to provide impartial investment advice or to provide advice in a fiduciary capacity.

Such a prohibition would affect your writing in important ways. First, when promoting an investment offering, you would need to couch it not as a recommendation but rather as something investors may wish to explore, examine, or consider in keeping with their individual risk tolerances, return objectives, and financial goals.

Second, if you want to provide meaningful viewpoints or substantive commentary on a particular investment, you'll need to do so without explicitly steering an investor toward a specific investment, as in the following examples:

Not Compliant:	Compliant:
In the current environment, **we recommend** investing in bonds rather than stocks.	In the current environment, **we favor** bonds over stocks.
We think investors should increase their exposure to asset-backed securities.	**We are overweight** on asset-backed securities.

Not Compliant:	Compliant:
We suggest that investors position their portfolios for a potential rally in the pharmaceutical sector.	We suspect the pharmaceutical sector is poised for a rally.

On a related note, your firm may be subject to limitations on publishing research reports that analyze individual securities in detail and provide reasonably sufficient information on which to base an investment decision. To shape your editorial agenda, find out what would qualify as such a report and whether your firm is authorized to issue one. The United States (SEC), for example, does *not* consider the following—among several other communications—to constitute a research report:[2]

- Discussions of broad-based indices
- Commentaries on economic, political, or market conditions
- Technical analyses concerning the demand and supply for a sector, index, or industry based on trading volume and price
- Statistical summaries of multiple companies' financial data, including listings of current ratings
- Recommendations regarding increasing or decreasing holdings in particular industries or sectors

SOCIAL (MEDIA) BUTTERFLIES ARE NOT EXEMPT FROM REGULATORY REQUIREMENTS

With social media gaining popularity as a communication tool in the investment industry, regulators and companies have adopted rules governing its use. In addition to the standard legal requirements for all external communications that apply to posts and tweets, you may need to conform to more specific policies, which can vary by firm and jurisdiction. Some firms, for example, allow employees to share, retweet, or register "like" comments on posted material (such as on LinkedIn or Facebook) so long as they do not add extra commentary trying to sway opinions—and only if the material in question has been approved as legally compliant for publishing and is already featured on any of the firm's digital properties.

You may need to abide by additional rules—such as with regard to creating, altering, or uploading content—depending on whether you use social media for personal purposes or are authorized to conduct firm business on it.

CONSULT A LEGAL SPECIALIST WHEN WRITING ABOUT INVESTMENT PERFORMANCE

You may need one before you even begin to write. Typically, addressing your investment performance—and comparing it to that of benchmarks or peers, as when discussing your rankings—entails a raft of requirements to ensure an ethical and transparent representation of past results (which, as the disclaimer's cliché goes, are no indication of future returns).

Here again, rules may vary by firm and jurisdiction. Inquire about them—preferably while your canvas is still blank—and brace yourself for the possibility of having to make elaborate disclosures that would have editorial implications for your piece.

Consider U.S. requirements, for example. When comparing your fund's performance to that of peer groups, you must exhibit a comparison of returns not just across one period, but multiple—such as 1, 5, and 10 years, or since inception—and disclose the influence of such factors as fees, expenses, and dividend reinvestments. When discussing rankings, you need to specify the ranking category, the number of companies in the category, the name of the ranking entity, the length of time to which the ranking applies, the criteria on which it is based (e.g., total returns or risk-adjusted performance), and other parameters. When addressing retail (mass-market) investors, you are not permitted to demonstrate how your investment strategy *would have performed* had it been enacted on, say, a basket of securities years ago under past conditions (an exercise known as backtesting).

And there are plenty of other stipulations, requirements, and limitations to consider for these and other performance-related communications.

SEEK WAYS TO STREAMLINE THE LEGAL REVIEW

Front-load some of the work in the drafting stage to reduce the reviewer's burden and avoid bottlenecks toward the end in your rush to publish. Consider the following tips:

- **Legal disclaimers:** Maintain a running list of boilerplate disclaimers to use for predetermined occasions. Ensure that disclaimers relegated to legends, footnotes, or the end of your piece do not inhibit the reader's understanding of your communication. Make certain they are written clearly and printed legibly, in the appropriate size and typeface as required for their particular application, and within mandated proximity to what they're referencing. See to it that all references to past performance are paired with the caveat that they do not guarantee future results. Finally, confirm that the disclaimers, which commonly vary by audience, are appropriate for the constituency you're targeting, such as retail investors, high-net-worth investors, institutional investors, financial advisors of private clients, institutional investor consultants, or the general public.

- **Leveraging existing material:** Lift or replicate as much previous material as you can—or at least portions of it—that has already been certified as legally compliant for reuse.
- **Visuals:** Make sure that all graphs, charts, and illustrations are properly labeled and proportioned so that their dimensions aren't skewed to overstate a point (such as in instances of disproportionate spacing on an axis to exaggerate performance)
- **Periodic workshops:** Every now and again, hold meetings with representatives from your legal and compliance department to address recurring issues, set expectations, and establish agreed-upon workarounds for overcoming the limitations of prohibited language.

DIVERSIFY YOUR LANGUAGE

By now you have a sense of the most common ways to reserve, qualify, restrict, temper, and modulate investment writing to make it legally compliant. Avail yourself of them ever so frequently. At the same time, avoid excessive repetition of the same qualifiers and vary your word choices so as not to sound stale and monotonous. Here are some examples of words and phrases between which you can alternate:

For Stating Viewpoints:	For Stating Generalities:	For Stating Possibilities:	For Time-Stamping:
In our opinion... We believe... We hold... We maintain... We think... It is our view that...	Typically Generally Usually Traditionally Mostly Normally	Potentially Prospectively Possibly Perhaps May Could	Currently Presently At the current time Now Today

ON LEGALITIES, CREATIVITY, AND INTEGRITY

Those who enjoy unfettered liberties to express themselves as they wish may occasionally view legal strictures as burdensome or confining. They include the creative community, of which writers are a part (or, in the spirit of qualified statements, I should say *typically* a part).

That's not an unreasonable sentiment. But don't let "legal" get you down. View it as a blessing rather than a burden: an opportunity to summon your finest—in creativity and ethics—within the protective perimeter of the law from which we all benefit. In fact, the imposition of legal requirements should sharpen rather than blunt the edge of your writing skill, hone your sensibilities for nuance and subtlety, recommit you to the highest code of our trade, and make you a more astute communicator all around.

Above all, view legal compliance not just as an *enforcement* of rules, but a *reinforcement* mechanism for the integrity of your firm and the industry as a whole.

And with that, good luck!

NOTES

1. Charlie Rose, *An Interview with Israeli Prime Minister Yitzhak Rabin*, March 16, 1994, https://www.youtube.com/watch?v=8kCfqCHbFas&t=153s. Retrieved on October 28, 2017. See the time marker at 31:10.
2. Financial Industry Regulatory Authority (FINRA), *Rules Reference Guide*, 2015 Advertising Regulation Conference.

Epilogue: Where Investment Writing Is Headed in the Twenty-First Century

"If you enjoy writing, you're doing something wrong."[1]
　　　　　　　　　　　　　　　　　　—Stanley Karnow

For a *writer* to say *that*?

As a journalist and historian, Karnow researched his subjects assiduously and produced volumes of thorough reportage over more than half a century. Unless he was a talented masochist of a writer—and it sure doesn't look like it—he must have nurtured a zeal for the craft. This leaves one to take his statement for what it was—a word of irony for those who *do* enjoy putting pen to paper: *Writing is difficult.*

Investment writing is especially difficult. Trapping you between a complex subject matter, a blank page, and perhaps an intensely brainy and demanding author you're ghosting, each new assignment requires you to be—by turns—investigator, interviewer, stenographer, interpreter, reader, learner, wordsmith, negotiator, and alchemist. You need background knowledge in investments to understand the professionals who lack the time and skills to write themselves and rely on you as their verbal crutch. And you need to cultivate good relations with them, adjust to their preferred methods of working with you, accommodate their idiosyncrasies, decipher their logic, internalize their thought patterns, channel their voices, and telegraph their styles.

Yet it's precisely these difficulties—and the required mix of intellectual and personal skills to tackle them—that should encourage investment writers at a time when automation seems to be encroaching on their trade. Computer algorithms, as it turns out, aren't just taking on the traditional work of security pickers, floor traders, and financial advisors (read: index funds, automated trading systems, and robo-advisors). They are also being developed and refined to take numerical inputs and produce authentic writing—from news stories to commentary and analysis—the kind that reads as if it were actually composed by humans. Some investment firms are already using software to crank out written reports, summaries, and presentations.

While the abilities of automated writers so far remain limited to the kind of data-reading, pattern-identification routines entailed in report writing, there are no known theoretical limits to artificial intelligence or machine learning. The power of computers continues to grow obstinately, still holding up Moore's Law and defying expectations a half century on. Chances are, robo-writers will only increase in their adeptness and sophistication, and narrow the ability gap with their flesh-and-blood creators.

Have you assumed a hunched posture of despondency yet? Regain the vertical and consider this: The unique complexity of investment writing holds a promise for human writers, a validation that even software may have its limits, at least so long as humans need other humans to understand and explain the world *to* them and *for* them. The greater the complexity, the farther off a time at which machines will fully replace us comrades, if that time ever arrives.

What should investment writers do to forestall it? Prove their worth as indispensable business partners. Bring a keen blend of reasoning, intuition, and emotion to their craft. Show that they are more than just rules-based penmen—but imaginative thinkers, nuanced communicators, versatile professionals, and resourceful sleuths who have a singularly human sense of what makes their investors tick, their colleagues satisfied, their topics timely and relevant and worthy of coverage. They must be quick to learn new things at a rapid pace every day and then turn around to teach those things to others with efficiency and clarity. They need to be critical thinkers in order to dig beneath the surface, understand context, discern patterns, examine multiple perspectives, and challenge conventional thinking. They should have social and diplomatic sensibilities to be attentive to personal dynamics, identify organizational sensitivities, and tactfully negotiate compromises between what authors *want* and what they may not realize they *need*.

In short, investment writers should learn everything they can about how their jobs will evolve, and, to borrow CEO Shelly Palmer's philosophy, "become the very best man–machine partners possible."

They'll also need to adapt to the relentless pace of modern-day change that Alfred Tennyson Barron never imagined when musing on his eighteenth-century perch. "The old order changeth," he wrote, "yielding place to new." Except that an "old order" by twenty-first-century standards—at the rate information travels, technology develops, and businesses evolve—may not last for more than 24 hours before capitulating to the next day. Investment writers are both victims and beneficiaries of this velocity.

They are victims, not just because of those microchips threatening to usurp part of their jobs. They need to churn out more copy, faster, and in increasingly condensed form for their time-constrained, perpetually distracted recipients. It's an even taller order when you consider the more strenuous effort it takes—paradoxically—to write with economy. Blaise Pascal captured the idea nicely in his admission that he "would have written a shorter letter" had he only had enough time.

They are beneficiaries, because never before have investment writers had more powerful tools at their disposal to become effective and inventive communicators. Thanks to technology, writers can push creative boundaries and flash content instantly, across various channels. They can gain presence with their audience in multiple forms—static and animated, written and spoken, audible and visual. They can experiment with new ideas. Consider that, in addition to digital-publishing capabilities, many investment firms even have fully equipped audio and video sets that look as if they're autonomous broadcast-network studios rather than the creative-services arms of Wall Street outfits. (Surely, Johannes Gutenberg would have been beside himself.)

If our métier as investment writers is to lay any enduring claim to necessity, it is because of the human dimension we will bring to our work; the collaborative relationships we will foster to bring ideas to light and make them accessible; the technology we will harness for the benefit of clearer, faster, pithier, innovative, and more effective communication; and the exquisite prose we will write.

Markets move up and down. Investment opportunities come and go. Money is gained and lost. But the writer can leave a lasting impression among colleagues and investors while bequeathing something for the ages, captured in the Latin phrase: *Littera scripta manet.*

The written letter remains, as do the many words we leave behind. And they are imperishable.

NOTE

1. "About Books," a televised panel on writing, recorded at the Bibelot Bookstore in Timonium, Maryland, and aired on C-SPAN2 on December 15, 1997, at https://www.youtube.com/watch?v=EPnbse6DGVc&t=2s. Retrieved on August 3, 2017. See the time marker at 9:50.

Index